The
NEGOTIATION
HANDBOOK

About the Author

Patrick J. Cleary is currently at the National Association of Manufacturers, where he is vice president of the Human Resources Policy (HRP) department. A former federal mediator with nearly twenty years of dispute resolution and negotiation experience, Cleary spent five years as a member and chairman of the National Mediation Board, mediating high-profile disputes in the airline and railroad industries. Previously, Cleary was managing partner of The Brock Group, a labor and transportation consulting practice Cleary founded with former Labor Secretary Bill Brock. He has served as deputy assistant secretary of labor for policy for the Labor Department and also worked as an arbitrator hearing consumer disputes for the Better Business Bureau. Cleary is a recognized expert in negotiation and dispute resolution and has lectured on the topic at Georgetown University Law School, Stanford University's Graduate School of Business, the San Francisco Academy, and the University of Virginia's Darden School.

The
NEGOTIATION
HANDBOOK

Patrick J. Cleary
Former Chairman
of the National Mediation Board

M.E. Sharpe
Armonk, New York
London, England

Library of Congress Cataloging-in-Publication Data

Cleary, Patrick J.
The negotiation handbook / Patrick J. Cleary.
  p. cm.
Includes index.
ISBN 0-7656-0720-4 (alk. paper)   ISBN 0-7656-0721-2 (pbk. : alk. paper)
1. Negotiation in business. I. Title.

HD58.6C57 2001
658.4′052—dc21   00-56329

Printed in the United States of America

The paper used in this publication meets the minimum requirements of
American National Standard for Information Sciences
Permanence of Paper for Printed Library Materials,
ANSI Z 39.48-1984.

∞

BM (c) 10   9   8   7   6   5   4   3   2   1
BM (p) 10   9   8   7   6   5   4   3   2   1

Dedication

To Kathleen and Maggie, from whom I've learned everything about negotiation.

Contents

Contents

Contents

Acknowledgments

Had John Danaher never invited me to be his "show and tell" project at the Stanford University Graduate School of Business, this book might have never been born. Beth Green, then an adjunct Professor at Georgetown University Law School, helped me sift through the many scraps of paper and inchoate thoughts which were my notes and form them into a coherent presentation with a beginning, a middle, an end, and most importantly, a point. Professor Rod Kramer at Stanford was kind enough to invite me back for a reprise over several semesters. I later did the same at Georgetown Law and at the San Francisco Academy, owing to the misplaced faith of my good friend David Demarest. Later, Dana Clyman hosted me at the University of Virginia's Darden School of Business, for a full-day exposition of the subject. All of these kind folks, and the students in these many sessions, helped crystallize my thinking on the topic. At a certain point, I decided to reduce it to writing.

With the inexhaustible help of Lois Sheehy—on her own time, I might add—the first draft was completed. I then went looking for likely suspects—victims, really—on whom I could foist a few hundred pages of reading, thus testing the limits of friendship. I am indebted to them all: Dick Kasher, the über-arbitrator and mediator and a true *mensch*; John Samolis, then the chief labor negotiator at United Air Lines. I sought him out because he was a good guy and because he was one of the very best negotiators I have ever known; Larry Kaufman, the respected journalist, then at the *Journal of Commerce*. I respected Larry for his insights, his writing, his simultaneous grasp of the issues, and the perspective so many of us lack; Armen Janzen, then the chief Air Line Pilot's Association (ALPA) negotiator at USAir. I had worked with Armen and found him to be not only a good negotiator, but similarly insightful and generally in search of a better way. Finally, I conscripted a true civilian, Fred Strype, still one of the best and most creative writers I have ever known. He lent a non-negotiator's eye to this pile of paper and made copious notes which were sometimes painful for me to read, but which were—every one—dead on. All of these people added to the final product, and made it better. Frank Newton read a later product and was too kind in his assessment, but gave me a much-needed shot in the arm. As friends go, there are none better.

I should also thank all those from whom I learned much during my years in this business. First, there were some great negotiators: Samolis of UAL, Ray Benning of the Teamsters, no pushover, but very constructive and never lost sight of the goal; John Peterpaul of the International Association of Machinists, also tough, but direct, and ultimately fair. Corky Swert of the United Transportation Union was the same, as was Ron Henson of Ford & Harrison, a management-side firm. Finally, Sheila Thompson, then of British Airways, was smart and determined and knew how to put the deal above ego every time. Every one of these people had one other thing in common: their word was their bond. Among negotiators, there is no higher praise.

Among mediators, Maggie Jacobsen has her own paean in the book, but I'll thank her here. I learned much from Bob Brown and from the late Bill Gill. They were kind to endure my youth and impatience. Without preaching, they taught me much of what's in this book. Also, during my time at the National Mediation Board (NMB), Lois Sheehy found a way to transcend the role of Executive Assistant and become a combination utility infielder and guardian angel. I've missed her every day since I left.

Acknowledgment would be incomplete without thanking my friend and mentor Bill Brock, who's had too many titles to enumerate here. I learned a little about negotiation from him, but a lot more about honesty and decency in all aspects of life. As always, the lessons of the mind are dwarfed by the lessons of the soul, and I am grateful for having had the opportunity to work beside him. I should also thank the president who appointed me to the NMB, George Bush. Like Brock, he is an honest and decent man, and it was my privilege to have served in his administration. In the same category of great men, I would put Tom Donahue, long-time secretary-treasurer of the AFL-CIO, without whom I would never have been in the business. He vouched for me when he had no business doing so. For his sins, he has witnessed a life misspent, but forever indebted. The great W.J. "Bill" Usery, too, single-handedly introduced me to half the labor-management world, throwing his full faith and credit behind me, when he was only really working on a hunch.

Thanks to all the good people at M.E. Sharpe: Sean Culhane,

who was my first contact with the company, was professional yet with an exceedingly agreeable manner. He made my hard work easy. Project editor Christine Florie extended my deadline once, but not twice. She saw to it that I stayed on schedule and did it in a way that didn't make me feel rushed. Eileen Maass, the copy editor, made many edits, and all of them improved the final product. I am grateful to her as well. Esther Clark handled all the early paperwork and was thorough and efficient.

First books allow one the self-indulgence to step back and acknowledge those who planted the seed, who lent encouragement in the days when encouragement was in short supply. First among them is the late Artie Riel, of Fairfield University. He played the Wizard to my Scarecrow, and told me to write, always write. Because of him—and at times, only because of him—I did. I am lucky to be part of a very supportive family as well. My wife and daughter gave up many nights and weekends while I finished the final manuscript. A special thanks to my brother Kevin, who wrote first, and best, and who forgives me my trespasses. Finally, I am mindful of William Peter Blatty's acknowledgment in *The Exorcist*, simply thanking the Jesuits, "for teaching me to think."

And last but not least, to this man's best friend, Reilly, who stayed with me through thick and thin, and sat with me night after night, year in and year out in my study, through first drafts and revisions, never judging, always accepting, just happy for the company.

The
NEGOTIATION
HANDBOOK

Introduction

This book will endeavor to walk the reader through the world of negotiation and dispute resolution. It was born from watching some of the highest-paid professional negotiators make the same mistakes day in and day out. They were all intelligent people, but time and again it was all too easy for them to become wrapped up in ancillary issues like ego and saving face. In the process, they lost sight of the ultimate goal. Negotiations have collapsed for every reason, from typographical errors, to ill-timed news stories and shareholder meetings, and even to one negotiator forgetting to tell a joke (see chapter 4).

This book is written for negotiators, but the observations come from the mediator's vantage point. As a mediator, one has the ability to peek at both sides' cards, as it were. As a result, it is easier to see from the end result whether each side maximized (and minimized) its gain in the negotiation. In almost every case, one party—or both parties—failed to gain everything they could have gained from negotiation because they lost sight of the prize somewhere along the way. Some of the vignettes herein will seem silly or specious, yet they are all authentic, drawn from actual disputes. The scenarios are not intended to demean the (anonymous) subjects or make them look small. Quite the opposite—their jobs are difficult and they were earnest and bright. Yet even the most seasoned negotiators fall into common traps over and over again. Hopefully through this book the reader might peer inside the minds and hearts of those who have gone before, who tried mightily but who repeatedly failed.

I was mediating a case between a very large company and its largest union in the last week before the strike deadline. They were only a few days away from the end date, and only four issues remained: pay, retirement, health care, and duration (i.e., the term of the agreement). We were totally bogged down, and despite everyone's best efforts, no paper, no ideas had been exchanged in a day or more. Time was running short.

The union came to me, very worried, and said, "Look, we're really stalled here. Somebody's got to make a move and get things going. We're running out of time."

I put the monkey on their back. "Will you make the first move?" We had been talking for the last day or more about the health-care issue and about possible solutions. The company had made a bold proposal, which the union viewed dimly, and the parties were left far apart on the issue. Basically, as the current health-care system was structured, there were no employee contributions to the premiums, and the company wanted to change that. A huge emotional—and economic—issue of the day.

The union thought for a while, and finally came back to me to review the other issues. On retirement, they were still pretty far apart. On wages, they were a little closer, but that issue wouldn't fall until last. Why? Because it always goes last. It just does. I learned that it was one rule that wasn't worth bucking.

That left duration. In the company proposal, the contract was up for negotiation four months after the last raise became effective. The union proposed that the contract not expire until twelve months after the last raise. A mere eight months were all that separated them.

Ironically, the last raise was only a 1 percent raise, so the company probably could have taken the union position outright anyway, because they could bet they would wind up paying more than a 1 percent increase in the first eight months of the next agreement, but in any event, they had their position, and by God, they were sticking with it.

The union thus hatched a plan. They said to me, "The smallest issue left on the list by far is duration. The other three issues are huge. We are poised to make a major move on the health-care issue. If the company gives us what we're seeking on duration, we'll come back and propose basically the same health-care package the company proposed a few days ago. But we can't make the first move."

To trade such a small issue like duration for an enormous issue like health care was a significant move on the union's part, to say the least. I quickly called in the lead negotiator for the company, and sat him down with the union's chief negotiator. It was just the three of us in the room. The company negotiator was a seasoned veteran. He had negotiated contracts for large employee groups in several different industries. By all accounts, he was at the top of his game, the peak of his career, the number three executive in this mammoth company.

The union representative spoke first and laid out in a very matter of fact tone the terms of their deal on the two issues.

"We'll give you your health-care proposal," he said, "If you can give us the twelve months on duration."

The company rep paused for a few moments, then spoke. "I'll give you eight months on duration."

I couldn't believe my ears. Obviously, neither could the union rep, because he just lost his temper and stormed out of the room. The company rep followed him out the door, and started back toward his room. I ran after him.

"Are you crazy?" I asked him.

He seemed as puzzled as I was. "What do you mean?"

"I mean, they are about to give you the health-care issue exactly the way you want it, in return for a measly twelve months on duration—only eight months more than you proposed!"

"I can't do that," he said, "Just accept their proposal exactly like they laid it out."

"Why not?"

"I'll look weak."

He thought that by just accepting the deal that the union laid out for him—without "cleverly" jiggling the numbers, kicking the tires a little, that he would just look although he were caving in. He was right—caving in to probably the best deal I had ever witnessed. I was incredulous.

"You'll look like a hero!" I answered.

We stood in the hallway arguing for several moments. All the while, I was aware that the union rep was on his way back to tell his committee they were going home to prepare for the strike, that the game was over. I told the company rep that he was crazy not to take it, that he was being ridiculous. He finally relented, but under great protest. He told me I was the one exercising bad judgment and that I was making a huge mistake, but that he'd reluctantly agree to the twelve months' duration.

I raced back to the phone and reached the union rep pre-

cisely at the moment he was walking back into his caucus room. I told him that he had his twelve months duration, and that I expected him to keep his end of the deal, which he did.

These parties ultimately closed the deal on money and retirement a few days later, but I can attest to the fact that this one episode left wounds on the union side of the table that never quite healed. They felt that they had gone the extra mile to get the talks jump-started after a period of dormancy and with the end closing in on everyone. In return, they felt as if they had been slapped in the face, and it was only reluctantly that they were willing to put that deal together, much less the rest of the agreement.

Because this one "negotiator" decided to be "tough," he almost lost the entire ballgame. He was so bogged down in his position and in posturing that he damn near lost the war.

As you can see from the vignette above, even the best, most seasoned negotiators make some very stupid mistakes. From the outside looking in, it's very easy to see. It is not so obvious, however, when you are standing in the arena.

Some of this book is in the context of dispute resolution rather than negotiations. A negotiation in its purest terms is a dispute after all, no matter how benign. It involves two or more parties with a difference of opinion about the details of the deal at the outset. Necessarily, then, the book will move back and forth between rules of negotiation and of dispute resolution, but they are interchangeable. Only the vantage point changes: negotiation views disagreement from one side of the table, dispute resolution views the dispute from the middle or from above.

In short, there is nothing new under the dispute-resolution sun. All *disputes* share common pathologies, from the earliest differences between Cain and Abel to a rent dispute, to the Middle East, to the last high-profile strike.

This book will also endeavor to demystify the negotiation process as well. In everyday life, whether we realize it or not, we negotiate all the time, with spouses, children, coworkers, neighbors, and vendors. The process of demystification here is akin to a prenatal class, bracing the unwitting new parents for what is to come. Lawyers spend their lives in the courtroom, but that scene is intimidating to the layperson. Boxers spend their lives in the ring, a terrifying forum to the nonpugilists among us. For those who do not negotiate professionally, a difference of opinion about terms or the shape of a deal in any context can be intimidating and fraught with peril. The aim of this book is to describe those elements common to any dispute, any negotiation, and to impart some basic tenets to guide you.

One observation at the outset: Many excellent books written on negotiation endeavor to bring the reader to a higher plane, to more enlightened thought, to a Zen-like world where everybody wins. These are ideal goals, and the reader should be encouraged to strive for perfection in all things. However, experience shows that most of us inhabit a very different world, a more practical one, where there is some degree of "zero sum" negotiations (i.e., if you win, they lose). If you can achieve the higher consciousness, put away this book and never look back. Go in peace. However, if you can't seem to get there because the noise is too great or because your negotiating partner has you on the run, clutch this book to your chest and refer to it often. It will help you to hold on and to steer through the storm, to keep your eye on the prize.

Some have described negotiation as on a continuum from empathy to assertiveness. If you can live at the far empathy end of the scale, all will go well. However, especially in the labor–management setting, negotiations are an exercise in assertiveness. In these settings, it is often hard to keep your wits about you.

Many of the lessons in this book will either help you move the negotiation, the dispute toward the empathy end of the scale or help you deal more effectively when you find yourself on the assertiveness side.

To prepare oneself for the life of a negotiator, there are really only two appropriate disciplines: early childhood development and education and nuclear physics. Concerning the former, people can become so immature and insistent on "getting their way" that they become childlike. As Robert Fulghum's (1993) famous book suggests, everything you need to know you learned in kindergarten. The pettiness and the petulance can really be quite palpable and damaging to the process. For a mediator, it is akin to driving from New York to Orlando with two five-year-olds in the back seat. When they're not asking, "Are we there yet?" they're fighting. Mediating takes great patience, firmness, and a healthy sense of humor.

In the shadow of LaGuardia airport I spent most of one winter with a particularly belligerent union and a particularly intransigent company. We varied our meeting locations as I tried in vain to find the right feng shui, the spirits that might enable us to get a deal.

One day we met in the union's headquarters. It was a small office with a small conference room where we huddled. Although it was blustery cold outside, the conference room was like a furnace. Incidentally, a hot room is typically a mediator's ally in that it provides a good external motivation for the parties to reach a deal and leave. But this day it was not to be.

At the appointed time, the parties convened in the conference room. The company lawyer walked in wearing an Air Force parka and sat down. He, too, was a seasoned negotiator and a very capable lawyer. The union representatives came in and joined him and we began. The parties had a long history and they sim-

9

ply didn't like one another. It didn't take long before a heated discussion on the first issue erupted. The company negotiator had not even had time to take off his coat. He became so enraged at the union negotiator that he stood up and announced loudly, "That's it—I'm leaving!"

"Sit down" I said calmly, "You're not going anywhere." To make matters worse for him, I was sitting between him and the door in this cramped room. He could leave only if I moved, and I didn't plan on moving. We had a brief but tense stand-off.

Finally he took his seat again, exasperated. "Fine," he said, "I'll stay," he exhaled loudly. "But I'm not taking my coat off!" he added, dramatically.

I looked at him half in amusement, half in bewilderment. "OK," I said. The poor guy sat there for an eternity wearing his heavy winter coat in this sweltering room. It took all the self-restraint I could muster not to burst into laughter every time I looked at him, perspiring under that big coat. All I could see was a kid in man's clothing.

As for nuclear physics, the analogy is this: Recall your first class on the atom. Recall that before it can move up a band, the atom must *gain* energy and before it can move down a band it must *lose* energy. So too with negotiations. When parties change their positions, compromise, move down a band, if you will—or accumulate a series of moves downward—the move is very commonly accompanied by some discharge of energy. Labor negotiations can get quite loud. In more polite company, negotiations can take different forms. One party may become irritable. They may suspend the negotiations, walk out. They might lose their temper. But one way or another, the energy must be discharged in order for the move to be made. Not to worry, it's part of the process. (See, "Noise Is Part of the Process," chapter 5.)

I was involved in a negotiation between a mid-sized company and its union. On an annual payroll of under a million dollars, the parties were still a few million dollars apart over the life of the proposed three-year agreement.

After a recess, the company presented the union with a proposal that made nearly imperceptible movement in the direction of the union position. The union took the proposal and went off to review it, presumably to respond later in the day.

However, only a few hours later the union called me to say they were ready to respond, and I called the parties together. The looks on the faces of the union committee were grim. The tension in the room was palpable. It was clear that they were not pleased with the company's infinitesimal, barely token move. The chief negotiator for the union spoke. Until this day, she had been fairly void of emotion, but at this moment, she was vitriolic.

"We are shocked and insulted by the company's proposal of earlier today," she began. The adjectives and epithets then came in a torrent. "Outraged. . . . Disgusted. . . . A slap in the face to all your employees."

When she finished, she passed—no, threw —across the table four or five copies of their counterproposal. She reviewed it briefly and stormed out of the room with the rest of her committee. I remained seated in the room for a moment longer to review the proposal on my own and to gauge the company's response.

Incredibly, the company and I were reaching the same conclusion as we read it: the union had trimmed almost a million dollars off their last proposal. After the company had made probably the smallest move in the history of all negotiation, the union responded—after a tirade, of course—with a million-dollar move.

I took the lead negotiator for the company aside. He was a courtly Southern gentleman, with an easy manner and a distinct drawl.

"Well," I asked, betraying no reaction, "What do you think?"

"What do I think?" he deadpanned as he scanned the proposal again, "I think if we piss 'em off real good again, we just might have ourselves a deal."

I had to laugh at the thought, but he was right. In this particular case, the union needed to make a significant move and they knew it. But they had to give off the energy equal to a nuclear blast before they could do it.

The truth is, like so many other disciplines, one can best learn negotiation by doing it, by observing it, by studying it. The goal of this book is to illustrate some common traps and to impart some do's and don'ts along the way. You might chuckle at the profound stupidity illustrated in some of the vignettes, but you should also see a bit of yourself therein as well. There but for the grace of God. . . .

One final observation on the nomenclature used throughout the book. You'll note the use of the word, "counterpart" or "partner" to refer to the person or persons with whom you're negotiating. This will be the only concession to New Age thinking in this otherwise zero-sum book. You'll read more about this later, but the point is to not waste time and energy, don't borrow excess baggage by thinking of your counterpart as your adversary or your enemy. But for the accident of birth you might be sitting where they sit. Presumably they have the same goal you do, that is, to negotiate a solution, or in negotiation parlance, to "get a deal."

You're in this together. They are your adversary only to the extent that they disagree with you on some details, on the shape of the deal. In the larger sense, the bigger picture, they're your counterpart, your partner. It will take both sides to get the deal. Don't lose sight of that along the way.

Reference

Fulghum, Robert. 1993. *All I Really Need to Know I Learned in Kindergarten: Uncommon Thoughts on Common Things.* New York: Fawcett Books.

Chapter 1

The Dynamics of Negotiation

More than anything else—yes, even more than money—the negotiation process is about power, ego, leverage, saving face, and, of course, "being right" above all else.

Power: At the core, every negotiation is a power struggle, no matter how small. It is one side's attempt at primacy over the other side's point of view or position. And, no one ever wants to feel powerless. Even police hostage negotiators know as a first tactic to create the illusion of power or control in the mind of the hostage-taker. If he/she feels powerless, the situation could erupt. The same is true in even more calm surroundings.

I was involved in a case between two warring professional associations. On one side was Group A, an association of very highly paid professionals. On the other was Group B, an association of state civil servant bureaucrats who regulated this particular profession. The average compensation of the professionals was several multiples of the average pay of the state workers. Group B could not seem to find consensus on a uniform set of regulations, so Group A faced a patchwork quilt of rules, which they found totally unacceptable. They were trying to force Group B to reach that consensus, but to no avail. While Group A felt a sense of urgency, Group B appeared to be taking their own sweet time. Group A was totally agitated and called me for advice. Before we met, Group A had issued a list of "demands" to Group B, which they were reinforcing through near-daily public statements. In between whacks with this stick, they would employ the carrot and try to ply select members of Group B's leadership with gifts and resort vacations. Money was clearly no object. For their next move, Group A told me they were preparing a massive public-relations campaign directed at Group B, a full-frontal assault, to get them off the dime.

"First," I said, "I'd stop issuing demands." I cited the well-known adage that it makes no sense to holler at a pig. It only frustrates you and it annoys the pig. In all aspects of life, Group B was subjugated to Group A. At every meeting, at every intersection, they were reminded of their inferiority to Group A. Time and again, they were quite literally left in the dust of Group A's limousines. In short, Group B felt almost powerless—almost. Group B had only one bit of power, of leverage, and that was that they set the rules that Group A lived by. Group A could spend, scream, pound the table or their chests as much as they wanted; Group B would work on a uniform set of rules when they were damn good and ready. The angrier Group A grew, the

*happier Group B became. Power. Having it for a change felt
good. Once they issued the uniform rules, they would never have
it again.*

In the labor–management setting, labor is used to taking or-
ders from management. During negotiations, they are on a more
equal footing, however, and can make demands of management
that they can't make in the ordinary course of business. During
negotiations, labor can hold up the sale of a company unit, or
delay a merger, or cause a slide in the stock price if they decide
to rock the boat. For the rest of the year— and in fact, once the
deal is done—they can feel quite powerless. As a result, there
can often be random exercises of power by those in a negotiation who aren't used to having it and who may not ever have it
again. Like a teenager behind the wheel of a Porsche, they find
the novelity both thrilling and dangerous.

Leverage: Leverage goes hand in hand with power. When you
have power, you have leverage. Leverage, however, can be more
temporal and fleeting. It often moves back and forth in the course
of a negotiation and can change from issue to issue. In a labor
negotiation, there's typically a balance of leverage overall. In
fact, in most negotiations, there is a balance of leverage. But if,
for example, you're in an affluent area trying to buy a luxury
car that is in short supply, you'll discover what it feels like to
have no leverage at all.

Leverage is a wonderful thing when you have it, and it's pretty
rotten when you don't. In most people's lives, there are only a
few times when they actually have leverage. It's inebriating.
Like our friends in Group B, above, they had leverage for the
moment, and by God, they were going to use it to the fullest
extent possible.

For the world's best example of leverage, we have to step

outside the world of labor negotiations and turn instead to the world of Uncle Bernie. Uncle Bernie is one of my many uncles. He is this wonderfully ethnic, great, good guy. All his life he had pretty mediocre luck, which is to say he had pretty rotten luck, but no matter. After retirement, he hit the mother lode of leverage, thereby changing his luck forever.

Uncle Bernie lives in Northern New Jersey, and like many of his neighbors, dreamed of escaping New Jersey some day. And so, many years ago he drove off several hours into the hills of Pennsylvania. Uncle Bernie bought himself a nice parcel of land. That is, he put down about a hundred dollars on a nice parcel of land and signed a loan for the rest.

Back he went to New Jersey, where he continued to live and work for more than another decade. Each month, he very dutifully wrote his check to the lender and crept ever closer to owning the land free and clear. Yet he never visited the lot itself; he left it out there like a dream that he only thought about. He wouldn't go back, he vowed, until he owned it and was ready to build his retirement home. Like all good Irishmen, he was a little superstitious, and he didn't want to jinx his dream home.

Soon, retirement was nigh. And so it was time for Uncle Bernie to make the trek to view the lot, meet with the builder, and decide on the plans for the house. En route, anticipation was high. It had been so long since he had been there, he even wondered whether he could still find the neighborhood.

Find it he did. As he drew closer, he could see that it was no longer the desolate outpost that he had visited more than a decade ago. Indeed the area had built up as the builder had promised. Finally, Uncle Bernie pulled up in front of his lot. There it was, after all these years. Right there where he had left it, just as he remembered it from the day he bought it.

Except that someone had built a house on it.

That's right. Somebody actually built a house on Uncle Bernie's lot. Somebody had made a major mistake. In fact, more than one person had to make a major mistake for something like this to happen. Among those in the deepest trouble would be a few lawyers, a title company or two, probably a bank, a builder, and some other bit players.

At that moment, as Uncle Bernie stood there, mouth agape, looking at his lot and somebody else's house, he became awash in leverage. I know of no other example in history where anyone ever had more leverage than Uncle Bernie at that moment.

As you might imagine, Uncle Bernie pretty much had anything he wanted from the builder. He built a beautiful house on a much better lot, and it really didn't cost him all that much. And he never even filed suit.

Leverage. It's great when you have it. It's awful when you don't.

Ego: Ego also drives many negotiations and lies at the heart of many disputes. Negotiators of all shapes, and sizes, and levels of sophistication have enormous amounts of ego invested in their proposals, their view of beauty. It is, after all, "my" proposal, "my" language that "I" wrote, "my" organization, "my" building, "my" house. Also, people like winning, however they might define it. To lose is a blow to the ego, and no one wants that. Negotiations grow more difficult the more the negotiators are wed to their proposals, to their way of seeing the world.

In any negotiation, the person with the smallest (or the largest) ego wins. In other words, those who are comfortable enough checking all that baggage at the door will ultimately prevail. Why? Because they will be able to see through the haze of ego to the merits of the various proposals, regardless of where they originated. Sometimes in negotiations, one side makes demands of the other as a sort of "love test," to try to exercise some leverage. They might insist, for example, that they meet only at a location that they choose. The egoists among us would bristle and insist on meeting at a place of their choosing. The best negotiators don't care where they meet or whose proposal is discussed. Their interest is in getting a deal, and they do.

Saving Face: Also tied up in ego and power and leverage is the concept of saving face. No one wants to be taken advantage of. At the end of the day, both parties must be able to save face. The more high-profile the dispute, the harder this is, which is one reason why mediators attempt to institute "media blackouts" in very public cases. Former Labor Secretary John Dunlop—a fine mediator in his own right—says that the greatest decisions are made when no more than two people are in a room. Even mediators must some times clear out and let the parties talk directly to one another, because they've been busy posturing for the mediator as well. They need to save face even with the mediator.

As a negotiator, it is very easy to become caught up in your own point of view and to grow increasingly averse to the point of view of your counterpart. This is natural—you are an advocate after all. In difficult or prolonged negotiations where personalities clash, it is easy for each negotiator to want unconditional surrender from the other. However, the best negotiators understand that it is their job to make sure their counterpart saves face. You need to give your counterpart a "back door," a way out, a way to claim even partial victory. If you do, it makes it easier to reach a deal on your terms, which, presumably, is your goal.

There is a type of face-saving in every labor–management negotiation. Once a deal is reached, the handful of union negotiators must take the tentative agreement to the full membership for ratification or approval. Typically, the union crows about its big victory over management while management remains silent. One reason for management's silence is to assure some degree of face-saving for the union, and it is wise for management to do so. If after every deal, management publicly boasted that they had carried the day, the union members might believe them, reject the contract, and send their bargainers back to the table to extract more concessions from the company. By showing some restraint, the company allows the union to save face and secures a final agreement, hopefully one containing some terms favorable to the company as well.

One final thought on saving face: at the end of the day, the tonic effect of getting a deal is great. Think back to the most high-profile disputes you can think of. Do you remember what the issues were and who prevailed on each? Neither does anyone else. Think of some of the most public major-league sports negotiations and strikes. On the day they end, there is a story about who gained from the agreement and who lost. After that story, the agreement is never mentioned again. The only thing the parties—and in this case, the public—care about is that there is a deal, the dispute is behind them, and the season can begin.

This is also true in negotiations over leases, buying a car, and so forth. In fact, ask those who've been through a divorce settlement how they feel when it's done and put behind them.

Fact is, issues of face-saving vanish in the glow of a final deal.

Being Right: "You must allow people to be right," said André Gide, "because it consoles them for not being anything else." There is no virus more pernicious, more damaging to decorum and peaceful negotiations in our society than the human need to be unassailably, unequivocally, 100 percent right. Forget food, forget water, forget love. At the top of Maslow's Hierarchy of Needs[1] should be the persistent human need to be right. The sad truth is that in negotiations it doesn't matter. *No points are awarded for being right.* Learn this and the rest is easy.

About forty-eight hours before a strike deadline, I was discussing options and issues with a senior executive of a Fortune 50 company. He was obviously frustrated with the union's inability to see the wisdom of his point of view. He wanted to know when he'd get a chance to go before some tribunal, tell his story, and be vindicated. But this was not arbitration, where some third party will hear each side and hand down a final decision. This was negotiation, where you must work together with your counterpart to find a solution. No matter, he was red in the face and was shaking. "But I'm right!" he kept shouting at me, "But I'm right!"

"That's great!" I responded as cheerfully as possible.

"Tell you what we'll do," I said. "Let's go find a print shop and have them make up a big button that says 'I'm right,' and you can wear it right there on your lapel for all the world to see."

I emphasized my last point. "If you want," I said, "You can wear it all through the strike."

I wanted to make the point. It didn't matter if he was right or not. He was two days short of the strike deadline. He needed to dispense with his obsession over being right and focus instead on getting a deal.

It's like the scene in *The Fugitive* when Tommy Lee Jones

---

[1] Maslow's Hierarchy of Needs, a theory by psychologist Abraham Maslow (1908–1970), posited five layers of needs, in order: physiological needs, the need for safety and security, the need for love and belonging, the need for esteem, and the need to actualize the self.

has Harrison Ford cornered above the waterfall, and Harrison Ford, as the wrongfully convicted fugitive yells, "I didn't kill my wife!" Tommy Lee Jones, as his pursuer, the U.S. Marshall, hollers back quite matter-of-factly, "I don't care!" His job was not to adjudicate his guilt or innocence, his job was to bring the fugitive back.

So, too, in negotiations. It matters little who's right and wrong. Those terms grow increasingly more relative—and meaningless—the more negotiations you experience. What's "right" is what the parties agree to. What's "wrong" are all those issues that keep them apart. No points are awarded at the end for being right, only for getting an agreement. Imagine a game of golf where you're not scored on how many strokes you take, only whether or not you get to the cup.

To put it another way, all the moral certitude in the world is worthless if you don't get what you want from a negotiation.

Drain the Swamp: One point about the end of the process, the goal. Although perhaps more appropriately filed elsewhere, there is a theme that has been mentioned thus far and will run throughout the entire book, so it must be stated here. Throughout the entire negotiation process, throughout the clashes of ego, the power struggles, the jiu-jitsu of leverage, the Scylla and Charybdis of saving face and being right, you must keep your eye on the prize. You must never lose sight of your goal, which is to get a deal. Recall the well-known adage that when you're up to your waist in alligators, it's hard to remember that your original objective was to drain the swamp. So, too, in negotiations, your goal is to drain the swamp. You must not let the other issues, the noise—in whatever form it takes—the distractions, the rhetoric, distract you from draining the swamp.

The best example of keeping one's focus comes not from a

negotiator but from a mediator, a former colleague of mine, Maggie Jacobsen. She and the great Bill Usery are the best mediators I have ever known. It is not often known that the mediator, too, bears the brunt, the ire of the parties (more on that in chapter 6). The parties often try to exert leverage over the mediator, too, to throw him off stride and to create heightened sensitivity, which might pull the mediator closer to their corner. Whatever the reason, mediators take their share of heat, and the same rules here apply to mediators and negotiators alike. All must keep their eye on the prize.

Maggie Jacobson is a federal mediator based in Washington. She has an odd mix of an easy and friendly manner and a tough-as-nails spirit. She is no pushover. A native New Yorker and former flight attendant, she has an elfin stature that belies her inner strength. Some years ago, she was working in San Francisco and was called into a particularly difficult waterfront dispute involving several unions. As is typically the case in a multiunion setting, one large union drove the negotiations. Maggie showed up and introduced herself to the lead negotiator for the biggest union. He was dumbfounded when she shook his hand.

"Who are you?" he demanded, "The secretary?!?"

"No," she replied calmly, "I'm the mediator."

He harrumphed and stalked off, making clear that he was unwilling to deal with her. She asked him to wait while she met and spoke with the other unions involved in the dispute. She then sat in a room with the other unions for some time, heard their concerns, and let them outline the issues and where they stood. When they were done, she walked back outside to meet our unevolved male.

He harrumphed once more upon their meeting again. "They must not care if there's a strike," he said, "if they sent a girl."

Now take a moment to consider your response had you been

in her position. Would you raise your voice in the hopes of blasting him out of the nineteenth century? Or would you just speak calmly and evenly, but let him know unmistakably that you did not appreciate his comment? Might you recite your credentials (and she had many) in the hopes of winning him over? Or would you speak to him, dignify him and his comment, at all?

Maggie did none of this. She calmly took him aside, out of earshot of the rest of the crowd. In a semi-apologetic tone, she said, "Look—all the men were busy today, so they sent me. I'm all you've got, now will you work with me?"

He was speechless. He sputtered and stammered and didn't really know what to say. In a moment, of course, he said yes— what choice did he have?—and the negotiations began in earnest. In a few days, they had their deal.

This is an excellent example of keeping your eye on the prize, on the ultimate goal. In this case, Maggie Jacobsen's job was to get a deal, not to re-educate a Neanderthal. Had she chosen to engage him, they might still be fighting today. Instead, she let the comment pass and turned it to her advantage. Her goal was to drain the swamp. She was never in doubt about the goal, never lost sight of it, and ultimately accomplished it.

As an interesting postscript to this scenario, in all future cases involving this particular union, the same union leader would call the office and ask them to "send that girl back here." He never became enlightened, but she was able to settle case after case with a very difficult personality, where lesser mortals would have certainly failed.

I was involved in a similar case with another unenlightened union negotiator (for a virtually all-male union local) and a woman (whom we'll call Sue) who was the chief negotiator for the company. For better or worse, this union never voiced their concerns directly to Sue, but voiced them repeatedly to me (i.e., *that she didn't have the authority to negotiate). They had never negotiated with a woman and were clearly uncomfortable at the prospect. Although they never said it directly to her, their actions made it clear to Sue that they thought she was naïve. She was actually quite a good negotiator. You'll see just how good she was in a moment. The union preferred to negotiate with another member of the company's negotiating committee, a man we'll call Joe. In fact, Joe worked in a different part of the company—not labor relations—and was actually outranked by Sue.*

We entered the last week of a long and protracted (and bitter) negotiation. The union doubted the company's resolve to reach an agreement and wondered whether the company was in reality merely agitating for a strike. As the mediator, I had no doubt that the company was trying to reach an agreement. Still, the union warned me that they'd be closely watching whom the company sent to the table this last week. Joe had been there only intermittently throughout the negotiations. Yet they had identified him as the more senior person (he wasn't) and the person with the real authority (he wasn't). They told me over and over again that if the company did not bring him for the last week of negotiations, it was going to be a signal to them that the company was ready for a strike, not a deal. After thinking it over for a while, I sat down with Sue and just laid it out to her. Sue was a great negotiator, because she chuckled and explained Joe's job to me, a very narrow and relatively low-level assignment. Still, she understood the "optics" and their importance. After only a few seconds, she happily agreed to bring him.

Sure enough, when he walked in on the first day of that last week, there was a huge sigh of relief from the union side of the table, since the company had clearly brought in—from the union perspective—the "big guns." Poor Joe ended up sitting in his hotel room watching cable, napping, and eating for the duration of the week. But it didn't matter, the union knew they were going to get a deal, and they did.

The big hero here, in my view, was Sue. She never became bogged down in issues of stature, rank, ego, and perception. Her goal was to drain the swamp, to get a deal. Had she benched Joe and told him to stay at home and tried instead to prove to the union that she had the authority to make a deal, she would have had a more difficult time. Instead, she made a surface accommodation, to send a signal to the union. By the end of the week, she had her deal.

In all negotiations—some might say in all of life—there is a bit of acting. Parties sometimes act enraged or indifferent, depending on the reaction they seek from the other party. As a negotiator, you must sometimes imagine that you are an actor playing a role, especially in some of these situations when the alligators begin to pile up around you. You must let the distraction and rhetoric around you fall on the character you're playing and not let it become embedded in your soul. This is an exercise, it is not personal except in the rarest of cases. Don't take these things, the slings and arrows, to heart. They are part of the process and you happen to be the one sitting there. Let them go, let them pass. Reserve time at the end of your life to get angry about it, but for the moment, you need to drain the swamp.

In baseball, there is only one thing for the pitcher to do: throw strikes. In the stock market, the rule is equally simple: buy low, sell high. In negotiations, there is only one aim: to make the list of agreed (sometimes called "initialed") items longer and make the list of unsettled (or "open") items shorter. Tedium is the stuff of negotiations, and you must plod through the issues. As you initial or come to agreement on items, no matter how small, you build a relationship with your counterpart. This is particularly important when the negotiation is part of an ongoing relationship and not a one-shot deal. The Japanese have a wonderful term for this concept, *nemawashi.* It means relationship-building and is an integral part of Japanese culture and business. They require much nemawashi before proceeding with a business relationship of any kind.

Coming to agreement on discrete issues is a key part of nemawashi for any negotiator. Although a long list of open items might lie ahead of you, you might want to step back periodically and look at the items you've closed and congratulate yourself and your counterpart. Of course, the less important items tend to be settled first, but these are no less important in the greater scheme of things. In hockey, all goals count for one point, whether they are picture perfect or ugly. So, too, with negotiations. Agreed items count toward the final tally. They make the good list one item longer and the bad list one item shorter. That's moving in the right direction. Initial your areas of agreement and build the relationship as you go.

Chapter 2

Preparing for the Negotiation

As with everything else, preparation is key to a negotiation. There are three things you need to do prior to any negotiation:

- Collect your facts
- Know your principles
- Know your priorities

Facts: In preparation for any negotiation, it is critical to accumulate as much information as you can, both empirical and empathetical. As for empirical facts, with access to the Internet, there is no reason why you can't be armed with as much empirical data as you want. If you're buying a car, there are hundreds of Web sites that can give you information on price and on the dealer's actual cost. If you're negotiating a lease, you should be able to glean from records public and otherwise what the going rate is for this space and what the landlord might have accepted in the past and under what circumstances. If there was some special deal that was given for some particular reason, you want it. If you're negotiating for a job or a raise, you want to know (to the extent possible) what others in the organization—or others in similar jobs in other organizations—are earning. When buying or selling a house, you can look at the "comps," the comparable prices of houses in a particular neighborhood. In a labor negotiation, you want comparative wage data for the geographic region and for the industry in question. An enormous amount of information is available on wages, for example, from the Bureau of Labor Statistics or the U.S. Department of Commerce. A virtually unlimited supply of information is available to you through the federal government and through the Internet. You should employ all of these sources in advance of your negotiation, so you're armed with the facts and so you can use these facts to make and bolster your case with your counterpart.

Those are the empirical facts. Equally important is the empathy. "Empathy" includes a person's or an organization's background, history, drive, motivation, mission, dreams, goals, "hot buttons," fears, aversions, hopes, and aspirations. First, get to know the *organization*. For example, if you are set to negotiate with a group of environmentalists who are angry with your company, who are they? What is their agenda? Talk to colleagues who have dealt with them in the past. Check their Web site— you couldn't do that ten or twenty years ago. How difficult or reasonable are they? What have been their demands? What did others in your situation do to solve the problem, that is, what did others have to agree to in order to settle the dispute? Are they earnest and interested in reaching an agreement or only in grabbing headlines? You can't have enough information on the organization going into a negotiation. Without it, you're at a disadvantage, and that can have disastrous results.

I was involved in a case concerning a company that had been consistently ranked at the top of its industry in service. Indeed, they were known throughout their industry and even among the public as priding themselves on their service. Yet the industry was changing, and they had been under a barrage of attack from other, new, start-up, low-cost companies. This company could not match the prices of its low-cost competitors and still continue to provide the high level of service they were known for. And, the customers seemed to be increasingly driven by price. After many successive quarters of substantial losses, the company decided that in the interest of sheer survival, they had to abandon their high-quality service and compete solely on the basis of price. There was no announcement, no press conference, just a quiet move away from service and into the fray of providing the product at the lowest cost.

A few months later, they entered into negotiations with a large employee group that had direct dealings with the public. Having suffered financially, the company was looking for minimal wage increases and in some instances, reductions. The union was astounded. They kept badgering the company about their proposals, "How on earth do you expect us to continue to provide the high level of service to our customers with wages like these?"

It struck me as I watched this negotiation that somehow the change in company culture and strategy had not been communicated to the union, or the union simply hadn't done its home-

work. In either event, the result was the same: They were continually talking past one another. They were working from completely different assumptions. The company was now a low-cost company, and the union was still trying to represent a high-service delivery company. This particular negotiation ended in a lengthy strike, in part due to the enormous gulf between the parties' understandings and expectations when they first came to the table.

In the above case, the union neglected to do—or chose to ignore—their homework on the strategies and aspirations of the organization.

Negotiators must also glean as much information as they can about the *personalities* involved and their motivations as well.

In one case, the company negotiating committee consisted of three people. The top negotiator held the title of vice president, but had loudly aspired to be senior vice president, a job that was vacant at the time. The other two people at the table, who both worked for him, aspired to his job, should he succeed in his ascension, as seemed likely. Incidentally, like most, this was not a company where one moved up the ladder by being known as a pushover for the union's demands. Consequently, as the negotiation unfolded, there was a battle among the three of them to prove who was toughest. The VP figured he'd never attain senior VP status by giving in to the union. The two underlings wanted to prove to him that they could be as tough as he was and that they were not the kind to back down to the union, either, and thus were worthy of assuming his job when the time arrived. It was like a testosterone contest. No one I could talk to on the company side would show a scintilla of reasonableness. They were all hard-liners trying to out-hardline one another. Understanding the aspirations of the three members of the company committee didn't make the negotiation go any more smoothly, but it certainly made it easier to understand the dynamics at the table each day, and that was enough of an advantage.

As with the organization, before you begin a significant negotiation, find out everything you can about your counterparts. Talk to people who know them or have dealt with them before. Are they aspiring to a bigger job and do they hope to use this negotiation to get there? Are they leaving the organization and have their eye off the ball? Many a good deal has been seized upon by people across the table from one who is departing their company. What is this person's temperament? Is he swayed by numbers or intangibles? Are you buying a house from a couple who has lived there for forty years and who really doesn't want to part with it, or from someone who's been there for two years, is in a messy divorce, and just wants to unload it, even at a loss? To the extent possible, find out everything you can about the person who will be sitting across the table from you. The knowledge will serve you well in the long run. You'll see in chapter 3 on "The Basics of Conflict Resolution" that setting the tone and finding common ground are important first elements. It will be easier to do that if you know something about your counterpart before you arrive.

Principles: As important as collecting your facts on a particular negotiation is knowing your own principles. Groucho Marx had a great line. He said, "Those are my principles. . . . And if you don't like those, I've got others." Don't fall into the same trap. Know what your principles are and what can and cannot be compromised.

Principles ought not be confused with positions. You'll have a position, for example, in the labor–management context, that you'll offer only a 2 percent raise. In truth you know you can probably go to 3 percent or maybe even 3½ percent. So your offer of 2 percent is a position.

Your principle may be that, as in the airline industry, the three major groups are stratified according to pay. The pilots earn the most, as a group, the mechanics next, and the flight attendants after that. If you leapfrog the mechanics past the pilots in pay, you'll have revolution. That stratification is a principle, it's immutable.

Add an important caveat to the above rule: reaffirm those principles periodically with the next person up the food chain from you. Graveyards and unemployment lines are full of people who fought for their principles long after their leaders had abandoned the fight. You might not need to check every day, but you should reaffirm your principles occasionally, just to make sure you're still carrying the full faith and credit of whoever it is you represent. If you're representing yourself, you should still periodically reflect and take stock to see if there is still reason or merit to defending the principles you set out to defend. Has time, circumstances, or technology changed the shape of the world in such a way that you should reassess? Possibly. Periodic review of your principles will ensure that you are always fighting a battle that's still worth fighting.

Priorities: Once you establish your principles, go to work on your priorities. The principles are your commandments, they are the rules, the parameters that will guide you through the negotiation. Your priorities are a more malleable list. For ease of reference you should divide your priorities into two lists: the items you'd like to have from a negotiation and the items you must have as part of the final deal. We'll call the first list your "Wannas," since these are things you "wanna" have, and the second list your "Gottas," since they are the things you've "gotta" have. The former defines the universe of possibilities; the latter defines your immediate goals.

As part of your preparation, spend some time to brainstorm and think about the universe of possibilities that you might want to gain from the negotiation. If you're buying a car, you know you want transportation and may even know the precise model you want, but what other amenities might you like? A CD changer? Four-wheel drive? An extended warranty? If you've decided on buying a certain house, what might you like from the seller? In a labor negotiation, management knows it must keep costs under a certain number. But if you're able to do that, what else might you want? Are there problematical work rules that have been giving you headaches in the past? If so, put them on your "wanna" list. So, too, for labor they have an idea of what level of increase they might be seeking in pay, but might they want to go a little beyond that if possible? Might they obtain a 401(k) plan, if they don't already have one? That is, both management and labor need some core elements in order to go back and sell a proposal to their superiors or their membership, respectively. Beyond those elements, what else might be on that wish list? You should have that list ready. The idea really is to dream up the entire world of possibilities, but remember they are only possibilities.

Take that list and make three categories. The first should be rather small, and it is the list of your "gottas," the things you absolutely must have from this negotiation. The next two categories are "wannas," what we'll call Tier I and Tier II. Tier I will consist of the issues that might well be in your proposal and qualify as things you'd sure like to have as part of a final agreement, but you won't be fired if they're not there. The Tier II list is your brainstorm list, your wildest hopes.

The "gotta" and "wanna" lists are important for two reasons: first, they force you to prioritize. Prioritization is essential, or else you'll end up fighting to the death on every issue for all the reasons and issues covered earlier (because they are your ideas, your proposals, etc.). At a certain point, if all issues are vitally important, none is vitally important. To need everything is to need nothing. You can easily become the negotiator who cried "Wolf" when you find yourself in a full-court press on a slew of items from your wanna list and then turn to a gotta with the same volume and intensity. For your own purposes, it is a critically important exercise to separate out the issues and the priorities, and let that guide you.

Second, you can buy gottas with wannas. That is, if you have a clear idea of what it is you need from an agreement and what items are expendable, you should be able to negotiate accordingly. Go ahead and give in on a few wannas and let your counterpart know you're making a concession in the interest of getting an agreement, but remind them of it when it comes around to your next gotta. In fact, if you want, you can try to tie them together, that is, package a wanna or two in order to get a gotta from them in return.

This may seem obvious in the calm and cool of reading this book, but it cannot be overemphasized. In the heat of battle, unless you've made your list, in almost every instance negotiators become so bogged down in all the atmospherics and all the ancillary issues that they find themselves arguing with all their energy about relatively meaningless items. Don't expend your energy or your capital—political, financial, or otherwise—unless it's to buy something you really need.

Think of it this way: if you walk into Sam's Club or Costco without a shopping list, you will inevitably walk out of there with the five-pound jar of mustard and the twenty-pound bag of paprika, just because you were caught up in the frenzy of discount buying. Make a list of your priorities and stick to it.

Chapter 3

The Basics of Conflict Resolution

OK, you've done your homework. You are sensitized to issues of ego, you are determined not to be obsessed with being right, and you are clear about your goal (i.e., getting a deal). You also have done your research. You know everything there is to know about your counterparts and their organization. You have reams of empirical data—you even know the names of their kids. You have a clear sense of your principles and your priorities. You have your two lists, one labeled "Gottas" and the other labeled, "Wannas." You are ready.

Now you walk into a room with your counterpart and it becomes immediately clear that you are separated by a wide gulf.

This is the stuff of negotiations. It is a conflict. The room is not yet crackling with tension, but it's a little awkward. You both are polite, but the cold, harsh reality sinks in that you want very different things from this negotiation. "I hate conflict" is a common refrain, and you do, but here you sit, right in the middle of one. If there is more than one person from each side at the negotiation, the sense of conflict, the potential for personality clashes expands exponentially. What to do?

Set the Tone: It is your job as a negotiator to set the tone of the negotiation. Do everything in your power to lessen the natural barriers that exist. You should be open, friendly, earnest. Some mediators sit the parties together on the same side of the table, while the mediator sits across from them. It helps dramatize physically that the parties are in this together. As a negotiator, don't be afraid to use "we," as in, "we have some difficult issues to solve," or acknowledging that "we" have a problem, if that is true. Some of the best negotiators employ this tactic, and it is very useful, calming, and sincere. In many—if not most—negotiations, you are tied together with your counterpart at some level and you—collectively—*do* have a problem to solve.

You might also employ the age-old power of positive thinking, that is, you might express to your counterpart your confidence that you'll work out your differences and get a deal. If there's a gulf between you, acknowledge it. Let them know you are committed to reaching a solution and that you'll do everything in your power to make sure this deal happens in a way that leaves you both satisfied with the outcome. Many negotiators either skip this important aspect or assume that the other side knows. They don't. You should make it clear.

Keep these points in mind not only at the outset, but throughout the negotiation. Like children, you must catch your counterparts doing something right. If they're trying, let them know you appreciate it. Don't be condescending, but say it. If they make a move in your direction, acknowledge it, even if it doesn't move as far as you'd like. Don't be a sycophant, but compliment them on their efforts, if real, to get a deal.

The most powerful example I ever saw of this principle was in the consumer setting. I was arbitrating a consumer dispute between the owner of an auto dealership that bore his name and a young customer who was having persistent trouble with her new car. There were only three of us in a rather small room. As was the practice, the consumer told her side of the story first. She was young and fairly unsophisticated, but was articulate and measured in her presentation. She told a tale of woe with many chapters and verses, of her purchase of this new car and its repeated trips back to the dealership for repair. With each trip, she grew more and more frustrated, she said, and felt that her concerns weren't being addressed by the dealership. For her troubles, she was asking me to order a "buy back" of her car, which I had the authority to do. She just wanted her money back and wanted to go to another dealer and buy another new car.

She finished her presentation, and it was then the dealer's turn to present his side of the case. He did, in a polite but firm tone. He believed he had more than fulfilled his obligation to this consumer. He confirmed her view of the facts, but differed on how far he was required to go to meet her repeated complaints.

When he finished, it was clear that the battle lines had been drawn. There was a conflict in the room. There were only the three of us, and the two of them sat staring at one another across the table. She said he needed to do more and he said he didn't. She wanted the car bought back and he said he would not do it.

Again, according to the procedures, the floor was the consumer's, to ask the dealer any questions she might have. I asked her whether she had any questions for him. She said yes, but wanted to say something first and asked if she might make a further statement, which I allowed.

She looked him directly in the eye. "I want to ask you a few questions, but before I do," she said, "I just want to commend you for your honesty. "I think both he and I almost fell over. It wasn't the least bit disingenuous. It was completely sincere. She continued. "You and I have different views of what your obligations to me are, I know, but you could have cut the facts differently, could have tried to spin them more in your favor, but you didn't. You laid out the facts exactly as they occurred and didn't play fast and loose with them. You're an honest man," she concluded, "and I thank you for that."

A giant sigh took all the tension out of the room instantly. You could hear all of us exhale as one. Both the car dealer and I pushed our chairs back from the table and sat back. A smile crossed his face. "You're welcome," he said. In one small utterance of a completely unexpected but earnest compliment, the conflict left the room, the wall between them collapsed. She never even got to ask her first question. He asked if he could speak and I nodded.

"I can't give you this year's model of the car you bought," he said, explaining that he'd lose too much money on the deal, "but what kind of car are you looking for?" Wisely, she wasn't greedy and knew a good deal when she had one and mentioned that she was quite fond of the next-lowest model and wondered if he might have one of them in stock from the current model year (a year younger than her car).

"Come see me tomorrow," he said simply. They shook hands and walked out of the room.

Had she decided to engage him during her questioning, she could have exacerbated the conflict. They'd probably still be arguing today. Instead, she sent not a missile across the table but a bouquet, and the effect was astounding.

So there's your lesson: Take the high road, walk away with a new car.

As a negotiator, it is up to you to set the tone of the negotiation. Your counterpart might not always cooperate immediately, but you must persist. The alternative will lead you to the basement every time.

Find Common Ground: Go back to the Japanese concept of *nemawashi*, relationship-building. It is the all-important cornerstone of doing business in Japan. It is very important to establish some relationship, some common ground with your counterpart. In the labor–management setting, it's quite easy in that most of the people around the table work for the same company. At some level, they all have an interest in the company's financial health, wealth, and continued viability. This does not always carry the day as we've seen, but it's a starting point and one about which people should be reminded. As a negotiator, you might have to do the reminding.

In another context, you might be a corporate representative negotiating with an environmental group that is threatening to picket or boycott your site. Good negotiators will aim to reduce the conflict by making it clear that they, too, live in the same community, share the group's concerns. Their kids play in the parks and fish in the streams. Perhaps you are an outdoorsman or a hiker. You have a stake in the environment, too. It is your job to let your counterpart know your three-dimensionality. Don't let them see you in just one dimension, to draw conclusions about you based on where you work or who you represent.

I mediated a case once where a few weeks into the negotiation we discovered that the company negotiator and the top union negotiator were both Harley owners. This was in the spring, and I think we figuratively drove down every back road in the area together with those guys at every break. It was something they had in common, and it gave them some perspective, gave them something to talk about and to focus on other than the dispute and the issues that separated them.

Do your level best to find the common ground that you—as an individual or as an organization—have with your counterparts. It is there in every case, and you just may need to dig or think a little to find it.

Repeat Back/Empathize: As part of setting the tone and establishing the conflict faced not by "you" but by "us," it is important to let your counterparts know you hear their concerns and that you understand them. When they share their concerns, it is important periodically to repeat them back to your counterparts, to let them know you "get it" and that you are working with them to address those concerns. As a corollary, you should make every effort to empathize with these same concerns, if your empathy is genuine. If a union is looking for more money, surely that's a concern that everyone can appreciate.

The merging of these two concepts requires a bit more skill and practice, but the idea is to repeat back concerns in a high-ground way and to couch their concerns as a concept to which everyone agrees. For example, back to the union that is seeking higher pay, the company representative doesn't need to concur with a 10 percent increase, but should empathize and repeat back, and couch it in terms of issues of economic security that everyone in the company seeks, both labor and management alike. It is a higher principle that guides everyone in the workforce. The same applies to job security, the opportunity for advancement, the seeking of respect. These are all laudable and common goals. The idea is to take discrete and concrete proposals on which you disagree and couch them in terms of common goals that both sides share. You can then work on the details together.

One final point on conflict resolution: don't impute ill motives to your counterpart. There is enough baggage around that table without borrowing trouble. You must begin from the premise that your counterpart is earnestly working toward a deal, same as you are. Yet time and again, negotiators see all sorts of demons and ill motives on the opposite side of the table. Don't fall into this trap. Imagine the best, expect the best, and most times you won't be disappointed.

Don't Let Your Counterpart Monopolize the Spotlight or the Microphone: This is added here because it is a situation that arises often in the context of dispute resolution. Typically the scenario is a fairly public dispute where you are being pressed (or attacked) by a person or group with a list of demands. It is a common scenario for corporate communications executives who deal with hostile groups (i.e., of labor, environmentalists, share holders, etc.). They often ask for advice on how best to defuse the situation. The first and best thing you can do if you have a loud and visible opponent—who craves the spotlight and the microphone—is to get others in that spotlight and in front of that microphone. "Others" does not imply people averse to your counterpart's point of view, although if you can get them more air time you should do it. Rather, you need to find other groups who share your counterpart's agenda but who are infinitely more reasonable to deal with.

A very difficult labor dispute involved three unions and one company. One of the union leaders was leading all the efforts against the company. He intimidated the company and the other two unions as well. It was a very high profile and public dispute, and this man was a media darling. He was always good for a vitriolic quote or sound bite. The other unions were so cowed, they wouldn't even surface. When we (the mediators) became involved, the first thing we realized was that we had to expand the aperture, as it were, and get the other unions involved. All our meetings were joint, that is, with all three unions. After the putative "leader" spoke, we would look to the others. At first, they were reluctant to speak, but after a while they found their voices and became very willing to be engaged in the process, and they were very constructive. Ultimately, by the end of the dispute, they had built an agreement, and the once and powerful "leader" was left to go along with it. By that point, he was but one voice of three. We refused to let him dictate to us and to the process. Once he went from 100 percent control to 33 percent control, the dispute was solved.

This can also happen in nonlabor—but similarly public and high profile—disputes.

I had a friend who worked for a large organization that was targeted for protest by a group of community activists, who complained that the organization was not hiring enough minorities. The organization felt the criticism was unfair and had met with the group. Once they met, they realized the group had a litany of demands, including a payment to them of several hundred thousand dollars for a purpose that was unclear to the organization. The organization called me for advice about how best to settle the dispute.

This was a large national organization with a strong presence in many major cities and roots all its own throughout the inner city and minority communities. They had some very good relationships with several African American churches and had done much to foster the cause of minority youth hiring, train-ing, and advancement. Yet this was not having any effect on the group that was demanding a ransom in order to lift its protest.

I suggested they pull together a group of their minority allies—all of whom were ideological allies of the protesting group—and bring them into the process. Whatever deal might be good enough for that group should be good enough for the protesters. Also, we knew that their allies would not demand a ransom. The ransom was really only to aggrandize this particular group. It had almost nothing to do with their alleged complaint against the organization. By putting others in that spotlight with the protesting group, by expanding the aperture to include others of like mind, but who were eminently more reasonable, it made the problem easier to solve. Once the protesters found themselves sharing the microphone with others (who were sympathetic to the organization, too), the steam went out of the protest. At that point it became clear to every neutral observer that the protesters were interested in something more than their surface demands.

If you find yourself besieged in a public dispute by a group with a particular point of view, find others with that point of view but with whom you can deal and include them in the process. They will serve as a leveling agent and can help bring the objecting party into the fold.

Chapter 4

The Negotiation

When you begin the actual negotiation, there is one central question you must ask yourself: Is this an ongoing relationship? That is, is this someone or some group with whom you will be—or hope to be—negotiating again? If so, all the following rules apply. If not, if this is a one-shot deal, a stand-alone negotiation, go for broke. Still keep in mind all the points about the stuff of negotiations, but as far as any of the relationship building is concerned, not to worry. It is very rare that you have this kind of a case. This is a bit of an overstatement, but mostly true. If you're not concerned about building any kind of relationship, grab for all the gusto you can gain. However, in most cases, where you have to live to negotiate and do business again and again, take great care to build the relationship and to heed the points that follow.

In a Continuing Relationship, Take the Long View of Negotiations and Be Ready to Leave Something on the Table: It might seem odd to list this observation first instead of last, but it will help you acquire the right mindset for the negotiation. Again, this assumes an ongoing relationship. In your preparation, remember you have readied your list of gottas and your list of wannas. If you're lucky, you'll be able to negotiate all your gottas into the deal, but not always. Too often, parties panic toward the end of an agreement because it is not perfect from their standpoint, in that it does not contain every one of their most basic goals. Don't worry—whether it's a lease or a labor agreement, you will live to negotiate another day. There will be another deal after this and another and another. For your next negotiation start a file containing the elements you may not have included in this one. If experience is any indicator, nine times out of ten you'll drop the item from your list by the time the next negotiation rolls around.

"Leaving something on the table" is negotiation parlance for not taking every cent out of a negotiation that you might have been able to take. It's not all bad—not a sign of weakness, heaven forbid—to leave something on the table, because your counterpart will likely remember this the next time you sit down to negotiate. It is an enormous show of good faith and it helps in the all-important relationship building. You need to keep this in mind as you begin a negotiation. Don't be in such a hurry—this is a marathon, not a sprint. To illustrate the concept, we'll use the example of someone who took the opposite view, who was less concerned with the relationship than he was with wringing every cent out of his counterpart.

This case involved a difficult and protracted negotiation covering literally hundreds of issues. In the closing hours, it looked

47

as if a strike was inevitable, but the parties managed to pull back from the brink at the last minute and conclude a deal—or so they thought. It is hard to explain the mood at the twelfth hour, but people are exhausted. Typically, they have gained much but given much. Any optimism over reaching a deal is tempered by the feeling that "buyer's remorse" could kick in at any minute if the deal isn't initialed and the whole thing can go south.

The final move in this case was a major concession on the union's part on a critical issue, making what was believed to be the final compromise for the deal. So many issues had been settled and the top union negotiator and company negotiator had been talking directly in the closing hours. Nearly every item had been reduced to writing and "initialed" (i.e., signed off by representatives from both sides). Everyone involved believed there was a deal on wages, too. Both sides had discussed it and thought there was a deal in principle—everyone except the company negotiator, that is. In going over the last details of the deal at the final hour, the company negotiator came back to the union to reduce the almost-agreed-to 3 percent wage increase in the last year of the contract to 2 percent.

The union was steamed, but they were at the strike deadline and so many issues had been settled that they weren't about to strike over a 1 percent difference in the last year of the agreement, and the company knew it. The principals from each side had a long chat, but the company negotiator insisted on it. The union was outraged, but they relented. They walked away from the negotiations with a bitter taste in their mouths. The contract was ratified, but they never forgot.

Incredibly enough, virtually the same thing happened three years later, when they negotiated the new contract. There were new players on the union side, but the company negotiator was the same. At the twelfth hour, he did it again—this time on dura-

tion, the length of the contract. He added a few extra months that the union didn't want. Again, it wasn't a strike issue, and the company knew it and figured they could extract a few more shekels from the union. Once again, any tonic effect of a final deal was erased by this last-minute gamesmanship. It was all in the interest of looking "tough," of being the world's best negotiator. In fact, he was the opposite.

About a year later—in mid-contract—the company found itself in dire financial difficulty and turned to the union for help, as partners. Surely the company was obligated to honor the agreement, but they decided to plead with the local union to reopen the contract to give the company some further concessions in an effort to help ease their financial crisis. If the union did not agree, cuts would have to be made elsewhere. The company's chosen messenger, of course, was the top human-resources person, the same lead negotiator. What do you think the union's reply was? They were still smarting. The company then appealed to the international union, but by this time, the man who had been the local union negotiator in those first negotiations had moved into the leadership of the international union. He had almost no inclination to be sympathetic or to help. Negotiators have long memories, and no one likes to be "taken." Because the company was unable to negotiate a new agreement with the union, they ended up making huge cuts in the management ranks and in other high-cost areas.

I'm sure some of those management people who found themselves out on the street as a result wished the company negotiator had given that last 1 percent, and had relented on duration a few years later. It would have saved a lot of pain and heartache and would have helped build a relationship that would have seen them through some tough times.

So take the long view of negotiations and remember you might not be able to gain everything you can in one negotiation. This, of course, does not mean you shouldn't try to maximize your gain out of a particular negotiation. Just don't do it at the expense of the next negotiation and ultimately the relationship.

Be Aware of the Signals You Project, or "Actions Speak Louder Than Words": In most negotiations, the negotiators become so caught up in the minutiae, in the nitty-gritty of the negotiation that it's easy for them to lose sight of the atmospherics, both large and small, surrounding the process. These can make or break the process, however. Negotiators must be assiduous about being aware of the signals they are projecting to their counterparts. Your inflection, your demeanor, your actions at the table, all have a way of projecting hope, optimism, pessimism, doubt, and so forth, to your counterpart. The signals are minor and are overlooked by everyone but your counterpart(s) across the table. Many a proposal has died not on its merits but on the signals that accompanied it. Beware, beware, beware.

I was called into a dispute between a very large company and its second largest union. They weren't at their strike date yet, but things had been only plodding along until one day they just stopped, hence the call to me. I knew both parties, but I knew the company negotiator better because I had had a prior case with him. He was a great bear of a man, a hale-fellow-well-met, a real mensch, and still one of the best negotiators I have ever seen. We'll call him Joe.

The union was pretty sophisticated, too, but they had been at this particular negotiation for a long time and were growing increasingly frustrated, and their membership was growing a little restless. The next day I flew to the city where the company was based and set up meetings with both sides, across town from one another. I met with the union first. "What happened?" I asked.

"Well," they said, "we've been plodding along out here, and we're not breaking any records, but we're making progress, and then last week we get this!" and they tossed a copy of the company's last proposal across the table at me. I grabbed it, but before I had a chance to look at it, they continued, "You wanna know how bad this [proposal] is?"

"Well, every day, Joe opens up the negotiations with a joke. Every day, he comes in, takes off his coat, sits down, opens his coffee, and tells a joke. But this day, he didn't even tell a joke!"

"No joke?" I responded.

"No joke! That's how bad it was! Even he knew it was bad—he couldn't even bring himself to open with a joke!"

While they were talking, I had a moment to peruse the proposal, and it didn't look all that bad to me. Granted, I'm not a party, but to my eye, it wasn't terribly offensive. I told them to stand by and I ran across town to see poor old Joe.

"What happened?" I asked, with great concern.

"I dunno," he said, apparently bewildered. "It was just the damndest thing. I put our proposal across the table, and they just blew their stack. They walked out. I was shocked! I don't think they even read it."

"Joe," I said, "What kind of day were you having that day—that is, up until you made your proposal?" After a few moments' thought, Joe recalled a particularly lousy day. His kids were sick, and both he and his wife had to get to work, and they were scrambling to get someone to take care of the kids etc., etc., etc.

As you might imagine, the last thing on Joe's mind upon arriving at the negotiations was telling a joke. In fact, he confirmed to me, he did indeed forget to tell his joke du jour on this particular day.

From the other side of the table, it was disastrous. It broke the routine. They sensed something was wrong. Something was *wrong—Joe's kids were sick. But they sensed his mood and felt it portended bad things. So when they received the proposal, of course, they didn't even have to look at it—they knew it was bad—they could see it all over Joe's face, and no joke to boot! Of course I got the two sides back together and made Joe tell two jokes—one for the day we met and one to make up for the one he missed the last time they met.*

They were off and running.

The above vignette is a comic but true illustration of how your mood or demeanor can affect the way your counterpart views your proposal. You can never completely avoid all such incidents, but being acutely aware of how you're being viewed— or that you're being viewed at all—by your counterpart should help you avoid this common mistake.

There is another important way in which actions speak louder than words in negotiations, and that is in another very common scenario when one party says they have no more to offer, but their actions belie their words.

I entered one particularly difficult negotiation, where enmity between the two sides was high and where over a hundred issues were still open. Most of the issues were union issues. The company was seeking only a few changes to the current agreement.

What the union was doing, therefore, was waging a war of attrition. They kept sending full proposals covering all 100+ issues across the table, and forcing the company to respond. Each time the company responded, they'd give a little bit on one of the issues, to show some movement, in areas that were less important to them. The union would take the company counterproposal, make a few small moves itself (again, on their issues) and send it back. For the union it was good sport.

By the time I became involved, the level of frustration on the company side was quite high. I didn't do anything for the first few days but observe. Each time the company sent back their proposal, they made it a point to say that this was it! This was really it! They had no more movement after this, so don't push us any further. This is it! No más! The union nodded, took the moves the company made, put them in their pocket, made a few tiny moves of their own, sent them back, and awaited the refrain.

Even I started to get bored watching this. But I didn't do anything about it until the company requested a meeting with me. Their anxiety was palpable. They said the union had come in with 100+ issues (true). They said the union was waging a war of attrition (true). They said the union was just sitting back, pocketing the things the company was giving them, and then just asking for more (true). They said that they kept telling the union over and over that this was as far as they could go (true) and that they had no more to give (probably not true), and then, in a crescendo, the company lawyer hollered at me, "I mean, when are they going to get it? When are they going to realize that no means no?!?"

I stared at him. "Not any time soon," I said.

Think about it. Every day for weeks and weeks, the company went in, gave a few goodies, and said, "That's all folks." That might have been fine the first time, but after ten or twenty times, people stop believing that this is it. I know the company negotiator believed in his heart of hearts that indeed this was it, but the signal he sent—unequivocally—was that there was plenty more to give. For all his protests, he might as well have said, "And there's plenty more where this came from" after each proposal, because, in fact it was true.

When you're negotiating, make sure that what you *say* is backed up by what you do.

There are many ways to send signals, from Joe's omission of a joke to continuing to yield ground after you've claimed you have no more room for movement. Parties also send signals by unintentionally creating false hope on an issue where they truly have no room for movement. Don't fall into this trap in the interest of trying to appear reasonable.

A large company had purchased a slightly smaller company and was busy melding the acquired company's employees into its own operations. With the acquired company had come a bitter labor dispute and a troubled work force. One of the inherited issues dealt with a plant that had recently closed, costing the company—and the union—some 600 jobs. The union had filed suit and had launched a wide-scale campaign against the company, its board of directors, and its shareholders to force the company to keep the plant open.

The large company—the buyer—called me for advice. The shuttered plant, they told me, had long been a money-loser. It was old and inefficient, with none of the new technology that had overtaken the industry elsewhere. It was clear to any independent observer that the decision to close was unassailable. In fact, the buyers were so convinced and so determined to convince the union of the soundness of the decision to close the plant that they hired a consulting firm to review the decision independently. The study would take several months. While the company awaited the ratification of their decision, the union continued to agitate. The company did not understand. Why wouldn't the union give up on this issue?

I asked them if they had any intention of ever reopening the plant. "None," they replied firmly. I asked whether they anticipated any report coming out of the consulting firm that might change their minds. "No," they replied. And, they added, there was no way this firm could reach any conclusion except the one that the plant should be closed.

"Then why did you commission the study?" I asked them.

They did it so they'd have some independent data to prove to the union that they had done the right thing. However, while the study was pending, it created false hope within the union. The union kept agitating until the study was completed, hoping it would reach the opposite conclusion.

Unfortunately, in this case, the company had to bide its time and wait for the study to be completed. In fact, its findings were as the company had anticipated. The union, of course, remained unimpressed and unconvinced. The study was intended to calm the waters by providing an independent voice, but instead it accomplished nothing but raising false hope.

Here's another example where one party didn't want to appear unreasonable, but also didn't want to raise false hope.

In this case, the union was trying to introduce a new and novel pay scheme into the company. The company for its part was not interested. They were willing to raise the current pay scales, but they weren't interested in adopting a wholly new method of pay company-wide. At the outset of negotiations, relations between the two were fairly amicable. Both made the effort of pronouncing their hopes for reaching an amicable settlement and working together. But the union continued to press for its new pay system. They came to me and said they wanted to allay the company's fears about this system. Since it was still early in the negotiations, they wanted to make a presentation to the company, outlining their new idea and its financial impact on the company, which they believed would be minimal.

I went to talk to the company. They were torn. While they really didn't like the idea of a new pay system—and weren't ready to accept it on any terms—they had a good relationship with the union and didn't want to anger them at the outset of negotiations by appearing unreasonable, by not even being willing to sit and listen to their proposal. Neither did they want to raise false hopes by sitting through any union presentation on this issue or creating the illusion that they were going to entertain this concept.

They really were on the horns of a dilemma. Finally they decided to visit with the union ahead of time and make it clear to them that there was no way they could agree to a new pay system for the company. However, with full knowledge of that, if the union was still interested in making a presentation, the company would be willing to attend and listen. On these terms, the union accepted and made their presentation. They didn't get their new pay scheme, but the relationship emerged without a scratch.

Be Aware of What's Going on Away from the Table: This is a corollary to the rule immediately above. It is another example of the importance of having 360-degree vision when negotiating. Your actions at the table speak louder than your words. However, there is a whole universe out there, away from your negotiation. What's going on in the world beyond the table can impact your negotiation, and you need to be aware of it. To the extent that you can control it—and this is an important distinction—you need to do so. If something is beyond your control but will have an impact on your negotiations, you ignore it at your peril. Examples of some different scenarios follow. We'll first address a situation that the company negotiator couldn't control but which the company certainly should have tried to control. The second scenario will illustrate a situation that was wholly within the company negotiator's control, but which he chose not to control. Incredibly, both these scenarios occurred in the same case. The third scenario involves a situation where the company negotiator had no control—and perhaps the company had little themselves—but where the left hand should at least have known what the right hand was doing.

This first case involved a mid-sized company and their largest union. Making matters worse in an already difficult negotiation was the fact that the company was financially in extremis. They negotiated for months, with the company trying valiantly to get the union's expectations in check. Still, the parties were millions of dollars apart. Every time the company made a proposal or responded to a union proposal, the company told again its tale of financial woe. They had suffered some pretty substantial losses for the previous year or two and the current year wasn't looking any better. No discernible upswing in business or profits was expected in the near term. Their outlook was truly bleak, and doubts about the company's continued viability were oft spoken—by both sides—and were real. Over time, this did begin to have some effect on the union. In my caucuses with the union representatives, it was clear that they were taking the company at their word and did not doubt its dire financial condition. They began to make some significant moves in the hopes of ensuring at least the company's short-term viability, and with it, their jobs.

In the last week of negotiations before the strike deadline, a member of the union negotiating committee came walking into my office holding a letter, his mouth agape. He threw it down on my desk in disgust. "Have you seen this?" he asked me, clearly agitated. I had not, but I picked it up and began to read. The letter was a nine-page missive to all shareholders announcing a special shareholder meeting for August 19, about one week hence. Incidentally, the strike deadline was August 18, the day before the meeting. The purpose of this special shareholders meeting—not regularly scheduled, mind you, but specially called—was to discuss the topic of executive compensation more specifically, enhancing the compensation package of their chief executive. The five-year package that was proposed in the letter would pay him *an additional $3 million in salary and $1 million in stock. The value of the contract they were in the process of negotiating with the union was estimated by the company to be $4 million.*

As if things could not be worse—other than the disastrous timing—in the prior contract, the parties had agreed to a profit-sharing plan that gave union members stock in the company. As a result, all members of the union were shareholders and thus received this special mailing from the company, broadcasting the CEO's new rate of pay.

Incredibly enough, when I called the company lawyer, he defended the letter and told me that, in comparison to other CEO's in that industry, theirs really wasn't making all that much. I was absolutely astounded at his abject stupidity. Not lost on the union, by the way, was the more fundamental question, how could a CEO of a poorly performing and struggling company warrant a raise in pay? He surely hadn't earned it by improving their performance by any stretch of the imagination. The company was on the financial mat, and here was the CEO being richly rewarded in the face of poor results.

I don't recall how we closed the gap in that case, but we did, partly owing to near-heroic efforts by the union negotiator and clearly in spite of near-heroic levels of stupidity by the company.

The above is an example of something over which the company negotiator had no control. This was done according to prevailing law, which required a special shareholders' meeting to substantially alter the pay of the CEO. Yet, in this case, the company negotiator—or someone on the negotiating team—should have known about the letter and the ill-timed meeting and should have thought the situation through, with all its unfortunate implications. At the very least, he could have given the union advance warning, a "heads-up," to let them know it was coming, so they didn't have to discover it on their own in the daily mail.

Now let's turn to an even more incredible example—if possible—of a significant happening away from the negotiating table, that had a significant impact on the negotiation and over which the company negotiator had great if not sole control.

Bill was the chair of the local union negotiating committee and was a company employee. Dan worked for the international (or parent) union and was there to help the local union negotiators reach an agreement with the company. Dan was being constructive and had been helping to move Bill and the others in the right direction, toward agreement.

One day, both the company and the union asked for a half day break in negotiations so they could handle an arbitration case, and I granted the short respite. Only later did I discover the details of the arbitration. As it turns out, a few months prior to the beginning of earnest negotiations, Bill had been part of a relatively minor infraction and was, with two coworkers who were more culpable than he, subject to appropriate disciplinary measures. The company had proposed a thirty-day suspension for Bill, half the period proposed for his coworkers. The company also proposed to put in his file a letter that would be removed only after three years. Bill decided to take his case to arbitration. Since he was a local union officer, his case was being handled by Dave.

Dave was a good and skilled negotiator, who knew how to pick his battles. He took the company aside and asked them to simply reduce Bill's suspension in half, to fifteen days. In addition, Dave asked that the letter remain in Bill's file for only two years, not three. While I can't reveal the facts of the arbitration, believe me that Bill's infraction was minor, and he was really only being punished because he was part of a three-person team that made a mistake. He was not the decision maker and in fact was the lowest ranking and least blameworthy member of the team, a fact readily acknowledged by the company. Yet the company adamantly refused to accept Dave's proffered solution and insisted instead on taking the case through arbitration—to let a third party, an arbitrator, decide the merits of the case.

Other than the previous scenario about the shareholder meeting, it's hard to imagine a dumber move. And it was not a mistake, it was a move intended by the company—they did it with their eyes wide open. They were a company on the financial critical list. They needed Bill and Dave to help them reach an agreement. This was no pie-in-the-sky theoretical issue, it was cold, hard reality. They took a break from negotiating, from trying to make nice with Bill and Dave, to go play hard ball with Bill and reject Dave's very reasonable settlement out of hand while they were at it.

How easy—and how much better—would it have been for the company either to drop the issue altogether (not out of the realm of possibility) or simply to accept Dave's proffered solution? They could have stayed at the table, and with noticeably better relations with their counterparts. As it was, it was hard for them to pick up negotiations later in the day with the same cast of characters who had debated yet another dispute earlier in the day. From Bill's perspective, the arbitration was much more personal. It also had the effect of making Dave much less willing to help bring the union negotiators more toward the middle. Time was running out, and the company chose to make things worse when they could have made it palpably better.

One important caveat on the above scenario, one important distinction: In labor negotiations—as in all negotiations—it is not uncommon for your counterparts to introduce issues over which you have no control. Most times, they intend to gain a rhetorical advantage or to put you off balance, make you lose your leverage, your concentration on that ultimate goal. They might even try to introduce issues over which you do have control, but which are not the subject of this negotiation. In the labor setting, outstanding arbitrations are a ripe source of mischief. If a union is facing a few dozen (or more) arbitrations involving its members—some or most of which they may lose—it is easier for them to try to get the company negotiator to wave a wand and make them all go away. You ought not do this, and the advice is consistent with the Dave and Bill scenario above.

In the Dave and Bill scenario, neither Dave nor Bill introduced this arbitration into the negotiations. When Dave and the company discussed the arbitration, Dave offered a solution, a compromise, but he never tied it to the negotiations. In this scenario it was completely in the company's interest to see the value either in accepting Dave's proposal or in dropping the case altogether, but they chose not to take either course. And—not an inconsequential distinction—Bill was the *lead negotiator*, with whom they were negotiating at that very instant! Dave was lead person sent in from the international union and was clearly trying to make peace. This is different from a union asking the company as part of the negotiations to settle all outstanding arbitrations or one particularly losing one from the union's perspective. This was not theory, this was cold, hard reality.

Yet it is not uncommon for the union to try to settle all their losing cases, and the company should avoid doing that (at least in all instances that don't involve the chief negotiator for the union). There is a separate forum for these disputes, and they should be handled there. You must remind your counterpart that the table is full enough without borrowing trouble from other fora. Negotiators often dangle a carrot in front of their counterparts, saying that they'll consider all these arbitrations once a deal is reached, and indeed they might drop all or some of them.

However, during the negotiation, the parties must not become bogged down by ancillary issues that are not part of the negotiation. Once the deal is done, talk about whatever you want, but while you're negotiating, try to stay focused on the issues at hand. That being said, if you have issues you want to tee up and your counterparts are foolish enough to engage you on them, fire away.

The third scenario is a simple case of negotiators being unaware of critical issues or developments in their own organizations.

We were gathering for a week of negotiations starting on Monday. On the previous Friday, that week's edition of a major national magazine hit the stands with a cover story on CEO pay. Ranked number one was the CEO of the company involved in the negotiation. I remember the number $18 million—almost quaint by year 2000 standards, but it was an astronomical number at the time. The union had all weekend to stew over it, and of course it made all the local news reports. How many times do you think I heard that number the following week? Yet, the company seemed completely taken aback. You can't engage the union on this issue (see below), but it was clear that the company had no idea that this story was out there and they were woefully unprepared to deal with it on any level. They should have known that it was an issue and that it would be raised.

Here is a similar vignette of poor news timing that almost threw the deal off course.

We were into the wee hours of the last night of negotiations. It was about 3 A.M., and we had been negotiating for days. This was the last day, and only a few hours remained. The company was reviewing the latest union proposal and so the union was just sitting idly in their caucus room, bored and suffering the effects of sleep deprivation. At a little after 4 A.M., the paperboy came around delivering a national newspaper. On the front page, there was a report that this very employer was making a multi-hundred million dollar bid that very day for a competitor. The union was irate. "If you can spend this kind of money on strangers," they argued to the company, "why can't you spend it on us?" Again, the company negotiators were completely unaware that this story had broken. Someone in the company press office should have had the presence of mind to realize that their negotiators were in the final throes of talks with their second-largest union, a pivotal group. Since the negotiators were caught flat-footed, it put us all in a tailspin and we lost a critical hour. Still, with momentum being in favor of an agreement, they managed to get a deal almost in spite of themselves.

One final distraction concerns your counterparts *introduction of* issues over which you have no control. A common one in labor negotiations is that illustrated earlier, CEO pay. Unless you control your CEO's compensation, you should tell your counterpart that there's no sense in carping about it, since there is nothing either of you can do about it. In a commercial setting, parties can introduce all sorts of ancillary issues into the discussion. In a real estate transaction, for example, your counterpart may complain about the amount of closing costs and all the "nickel-and-diming" that goes on. That's nice. There's absolutely nothing you can do about that, and you ought to tell them so. Someone else makes those rules. Why does there have to be a title search? There just does, and it's outside of your domain. If they want you to pay for it somehow, demur. It's not your problem. You must firmly and forcefully state this at the outset, at the first instance that the issue is introduced. Don't be angry, just firm. If you don't intend to address or fix the issue, then don't engage or indulge your counterpart in the discussion, to create the illusion that there's anything you can do about it. Nip it in the bud.

Probe Your Counterpart's Priorities: Since you've read this book, you will come prepared to any negotiation with your clean, clear lists of priorities. However, if your counterparts did not read this book (and you should hope they didn't), then they might not have done similar homework, so you'll need to help them through the process. Good negotiators not only give their counterparts a back door, to save face, but they also help focus their counterparts, and help them prioritize if they've been unable to do so.

In the rarest of cases, you can simply ask. On infrequent occasions, one party or another might be very plain, very clear about what their priorities are. However, in general, people seem committed to the more typical Kabuki dance of negotiations, (i.e., of hiding their true priorities, goals, motives, and intent). If this more common kind of negotiators are sitting across the table from you, you will need to try to figure out what they really need from this negotiation, even if they may not know it themselves.

In the labor setting, you are typically looking at a proposal that is hundreds of pages long, containing hundreds of issues. A boilerplate lease is filled with small-print paragraphs, spelling out every detail, both important and inconsequential. How on earth can you know which of these issues are of critical importance to your counterpart? The unevolved negotiators will usually fight as hard over the minutiae as over the big issues. From across the table, if the noise level is the same, it's difficult to glean their priorities. However, through some creative probing—and the use of a mediator, if you have one—you can test their depth of commitment on any particular issue. It is the difference between theology and economics, that is, the issues that run to their core and the ones that can be purchased. In any negotiation, the latter greatly outnumber the former. There are those cynics who would contend that there are no theological issues, only economic ones, but typically there are a few theological issues buried in every negotiation.

An illustration of the difference between economics and theology, between "no" and "hell, no":

I was mediating a case involving two union locals and a mid-sized company. The unions represented the same craft of workers, but in two different geographical locations. Technology had greatly impacted their industry of late, and mechanization had obviated the need for about a quarter to a third of their members. The company was looking for a way to downsize, to re duce the payroll, and to bring operations more in line with the available technology. The union, for its part, was intent on saving as many jobs as possible.

The company came to me and told me they were willing to throw money at the problem. That is, they were willing to spend pretty liberally to buy out those workers who were not needed. They asked me whether I thought it was worth having the discussion, or indeed whether the union was even willing to have the discussion. That is, was the issue theological or economic?

I did what any good Irish cop would do. I separated the two local union presidents, put each in his own room. Incidentally, they had made it clear to me that each had the power to make his own deal, although most of us believed they would settle together, less out of solidarity than mistrust. I walked into the first room to talk to union leader A. After discussing the issue for a while, I told him the company was willing to open its wallet to spend a little bit to buy out some of his members. He looked at me sternly. "No amount of money—no amount—will make me give in on this issue." He sat there, arms folded across his chest. Everything about him told me this was a theological issue. This is called a "hell, no."

I sat there for a moment and let his answer linger in the air, then walked next door to his colleague, union leader B. We discussed the issue a little bit and then I told him, as I had told leader A, that the company was willing to spend some money to make this issue go away. He, too, looked at me sternly. "No amount of money—no amount—will make me give in on this issue," he said, and he paused for only a moment. "But how much money is the company talking about?"

This is the difference between theology and economics. For leader A, there was no way he was going to give up on this issue. He didn't care how much money the company was ready to spend, he wasn't interested. His colleague, on the other hand, wanted just a little peek inside that wallet, to see exactly how much was there. Why? Because he'd sell the issue for the right price. It was an economic matter to him.

You need to try your level best—either directly or through a mediator—to glean from your counterparts which issues are theological and which are economic. If you ask, it's too easy for them to say they're all theological. You must prod and probe. You don't always need to use money to loosen the joints, but it is the great equalizer. If money doesn't do it, usually nothing else will, although there are exceptions. Here's another example of sorting out theology from economics, again using money as the grease.

This case involved a mid-sized company and its largest union. This case was particularly noteworthy because it was the first contract that was open for negotiation in their particular industry. Many others were in the queue behind it, so all parties had one eye across the table at their counterparts and one eye over their shoulder at the other cases that were coming. The other cases involved this same union, so they knew whatever they did in this case would set the pattern for the others.

For the company, as the first ones through the pipeline, they really didn't care about the pattern. They wanted the best deal they could get. Interestingly, altering the dynamics here was the fact that the company lawyers represented the other companies that were in the queue behind them, so they had an interest all their own in not giving too much away, lest the results live to haunt them in the other negotiations at the other companies with this same union.

One issue emerged from the union side as the central issue, the sticking point. It was a new concept they were proposing, one that did not yet exist in the industry. The union characterized it to me as an economic issue. They told me that their members would make more money once this concept was established. The company was not terribly keen on the idea, and their lawyers were stiffening their spines at every turn. I knew we had to settle this issue somehow in order to reach a final deal, so I sat down and visited with the union. They reviewed the issue with me again, and they again insisted that this was not theology, just a matter of economics, pure and simple. I should add that in addition to the local union, senior representatives from the international union were also present. They would be helping to negotiate the deals at the other companies as well. Their presence reinforced my suspicion that there was something more than economics at stake.

I made it clear to them that I was not carrying the company's proxy (i.e., I was not making or floating proposals on the company's behalf). My questions were the product of my own inquisitive and otherwise idle mind. The company had a wage proposal on the table that would have raised their wages 3 percent in each of three years. I asked them if they might drop this other issue if the company raised its offer to 4 percent. As Detective Colombo might say, I was just wondering, not proposing. They told me it was a non-starter. By the way, they said, that might not give their people the kind of gains they might realize from their proposal.

I asked if they would drop it if the company offered 5 percent. They said no. "What about a 10 percent wage increase?" I asked. This would clearly give every one of their members far more than they would ever gain under the union proposal as is. I doubted the company could go there, I said, but what if they could, in the interest of making this issue go away?

"Not interested" was the union reply.

It was a theological issue, pure and simple.

Use "What-If's": In the example just cited you'll see the use of what is called "what if's." It is, as its name implies, a method of tossing out possibilities to your counterparts. It is also a central weapon in any mediator's arsenal. It is the best way to probe the difference between economic and theological issues. You can employ it to probe on any issue, however, and glean a sense of your counterpart's depth of commitment on an issue. A few tips, however: You should be clear, whether you're a negotiator or a mediator, whether you're really proposing something or just wondering aloud. Many negotiators use "what if's" to float proposals. If you're doing that, let your counterparts know (if they ask), If not, if you're just wondering about parameters, make that clear. As a mediator, you must be absolutely clear that you are not floating a proposal from the other side. Otherwise, it would be reasonable for them to assume that you are.

The fundamental beauty of "what if's" is that you don't need to be constrained by logic or by any other parameters. You can honestly suggest relatively outrageous scenarios, to get some sense of the starting and ending points of their various positions. In the example given above, creeping up in wage proposals by 1 percent didn't seem to move the union. Jumping to 10 percent didn't do it either. You might say that it's easy for people to decline an outrageous offer, but in the above scenario, with the negotiator creeping up by 1 percent at a time, it was clear that there was no level at which they would relent.

In the marketplace, when you are buying or selling, feel free to push the envelope with "what if's." If someone gives you an estimate on home improvement, but says they can't start for six months, ask "what if" you paid a premium of 30 percent or 50 percent, could he start earlier? If he says no, then he really is constrained by other factors. If he says yes, then it's a matter of money and priorities. Those are issues you can work with. They're economic, not theological. Don't pay the premium, but work with the knowledge you've just gleaned, that is, be persistent, try to urge him to begin work a little earlier.

"What if's" are limited only by your own creativity. When you're stuck on an issue, in formal negotiations or in the negotiations of everyday life (i.e., when you receive a "no" answer) ask your own "what if," to see whether others' objections are economic or theological.

Be Aware of Layers of Interests at the Table: You may have heard the adage that when you're negotiating, you should focus on your—and your counterparts'—interests, not on the particular position. This is good advice. However, it is easier in the statement than in the practice. In real life, in larger negotiations, there are many layers of interests around the table. Let's use the example presented earlier, where the union that insisted on (what turned out to be) a theological issue. To the casual observer, there were two interests at that table, the labor interest and the management interest. Yet upon closer inspection, you see that "the union" really consisted of the local and the international union. Truth is, the local probably didn't care much about this issue, but the international needed it to establish the beachhead for all future negotiations in the industry.

On the company side, the company probably felt about the same as the local union representatives felt. That is, they just wanted a deal at their company and didn't much care to take on external fights. Yet their own lawyers had their own point of view, since they also represented so many other companies in that industry. If this issue fell here, they would be fighting it (and probably losing) with all their other client companies, too. Thus, they were working overtime to make sure the company didn't give in on this issue. A naïf on either side of the table might think the issue was easily soluble because they knew the interest of the company or of the union local. They would have completely underestimated the resolve from the other side of the table because of the other layer of interests that kicked in.

Also above, in chapter 2 (Preparing for the Negotiation), under "Facts" and specifically the discussion of "empathy," you'll see an example of a company negotiating team that was a veritable Napoleon of interests. In that case, they were all interested in being tough, but that didn't make their job any easier. From the other side of the table, they might have appeared to be a monolith, but that would have been a perilous assumption.

As it turns out, on the other side of the table in that same negotiation was an even more dysfunctional committee, if possible. That situation again makes the point about layers of interests. Keep in mind that typically there is a local union, then (in some unions) a district, and finally the international.

At one company, two local units of the same union were bickering with one another. Above them was one person who was in charge of all the union's workers at that company, including those in these two locals. He was a company employee. He had been elected with the support of one of the locals and without the support of the other. So in addition to warring with another union, one of the locals was warring with him. Above him was the district representative. He was also elected. The district included this union's workers from many different crafts, at many different companies. One of the issues in the election for district representative was that the district had neglected this company's workers in the past, so at this point, the district representative was trying to pay very close attention to their every need.

That would have been fine, but owing to some issues of financial mismanagement, the district had just been put in trusteeship by the international, and so the international sent a representative to monitor—or baby-sit—the district representative and the talks in general. I felt sorry for the international representative. He had flown in from out of town and was completely persona non grata. I violated every mediator's rule I had about not being seen eating or otherwise apparently socializing with only one of the parties. This poor guy didn't have a friend in the world, and so we spent time together. I had no fears about being accused of partisanship, since his own union refused to let him into their room most of the time.

As noted earlier, the company was far from a monolith, because of their many aspirations. On the union side, there was really no one in charge. Ultimately, the international had to approve any deal that was done, but the international representative had no apparent authority with his own group. The closest we could come to someone in charge was the district representative, but because of the politics, he really didn't want to be too heavy-handed with the locals. He needed their support and was there to show them, by God, that they had the full faith and credit of the district, in spite of their worst fears. On any given issue, arguments would break out on both sides of the table (i.e., the parties would fight among themselves). We finally reached an agreement, but it was due to sheer fortitude, persistence, and each party's sincere desire to get away from one another.

Ask, "Whose Interest Is This?": When there are layers of interests present—as there almost always are—try to be clear about whose interest is driving a particular issue. Once you successfully identify the interest or interests that need to be addressed, the problems can be quite easily solved. But the difficult task lies in identifying the interest that is driving a particular position. Once cognizant of the many layers of interests on your counterpart's side of the table, you must then try to glean the interest behind each position, each issue you are trying to solve. The following vignette is told from the view of the mediator, but the principle still pertains.

I received two phone calls about fifteen minutes apart, one from the CEO of a fairly large company and one from the head of the international union representing the company's largest group of employees. Negotiations had bogged down and they were trying to get them jump-started. Neither of them was at the negotiating table. The company had their chief negotiator at the table and the union had the head of the local union. The CEO mentioned no particular issues to me in our call, but the international union president used the occasion of our call to lobby me pretty strongly on the issue of health care, a particularly thorny issue of the day. He wanted me to "stay away from it" and said that they would brook no compromise on it. It was clear to me that as the president of the international union, he had a great interest in making sure this issue didn't fall. If it did, it would fall for them in all other contracts that they would negotiate for time immemorial. I gathered that he feared that the local union might be weak, might let themselves be bullied on it by the company, and he wanted a second line of defense—the mediator, in this case—to make sure there would be no compromise. He clearly drew his line in the sand on behalf of the larger group. I heard him out and convened a meeting of the negotiators a few days hence.

At that meeting, and indeed as the negotiations progressed, it became clear to me that the forbidden issue of health care would loom large and would remain a sticking point. A few days into these intensive, near round-the-clock negotiations, I called the president of the international again and broached the issue. He was irate.

"I told you to stay away from it," he warned me again. "We're just not going to compromise on that issue," he said again. I had my answer. The institutional interest in not yielding on this issue was again palpable to me.

In a very few days, we were coming to agreement on all other issues, leaving only a few remaining, but none as large as health care. During a break in the negotiations, I was making idle conversation with the union local president, their chief negotiator. Part in exasperation and partly on a fishing expedition, I said I wished the international didn't feel so strongly about health care.

"What's the international got to do with this?" he asked me, matter-of-factly. I told him that I understood that they had a strong institutional view on this issue.

He looked truly puzzled. "I have no idea what their position on it is," he said.

I told him of my conversation with his international president, and his face broke into a broad grin and he nodded. "Good," he said, upon hearing of the tough stance taken by the international president, "He was carrying my water." In other words, the international president knew it was a big issue to the local and wanted to do his duty as the head of the organization *by helping them to fight the battle on their key issue. For me, this was more than a minor distinction. If it had been an issue of importance to the international then it would have been theological and very difficult to solve. Once I realized it was the local union's issue, I knew it was economic and eminently soluble. Indeed, as my conversation continued with the local union president, he was very clear about his concerns (i.e., that there was no upper limit to how much his members could ultimately pay), and they were easily addressed, that is, through a cap on the amount of money the employees would pay for health care. We settled the issue in a ten-minute conversation.*

I learned a valuable lesson that day, however, about interests. Thinking it was someone else's interest, I made judgments that were completely in error. Upon figuring out precisely whose interest this was and what their rationale was, the issue was solved just like all the others, and our deal was imminent.

In the above scenario, the ultimate solution was easy. The hard part was figuring out whose interest it was in the first place. Below are two more examples where logjams were broken upon addressing in a very personal way the concerns of the precise individuals on the negotiating committee.

I had a case involving a group with particularly high turnover. However, a solid third of the workforce had enjoyed a fairly long tenure. As is often the case, the union negotiating committee was comprised of the tenured employees. That made them the exception rather than the rule in this particular workforce. One of the issues in the union's opening salvo was a proposal to greatly enhance the company pension plan. The company immediately declared this proposal from the union a "non-starter." It was their view that most of their workforce really didn't care about this issue.

This, incidentally, is a classic conundrum in negotiations. One

*side says, "This really isn't a problem, so why do you need this?"
and the other side counters by saying, "If the language will be
ultimately meaningless, then why would you object to including
it in the final agreement?" There is no solution, and there appeared to be none in this particular case. This illustrates yet
another common problem: In labor negotiations, management
is everlastingly making bold statements about a particular offer's
salability to the employees that the union represents. Unfortunately, in labor negotiations, it is the union's judgment only when
to put a contract out to the membership for ratification. Unless
and until the union negotiators and leadership are satisfied, that
agreement will not see the light of day. This, necessarily, height-
ens the politics around the table, as it did here.*

*In fact, both the union and the company had a pension pro-
posal. Despite its own protests, the company eventually came to
believe that it had to "sweeten" the pension plan if it were to
reach a final deal. From the union's perspective, the company
proposal was not "sweet" enough. We spent days arguing about
the theories of the opposing plans and their potential impact.
Finally, I asked the company if they could run the numbers under their proposal (i.e., show us the practical effect on a sample
employee or two). I suggested they use the negotiating committee as their examples, and the company complied. When the
members of the negotiating committee saw their own pension
performance, the company's proposal became easier to accept.
For a moment, the greater good went out the window and good
old-fashioned self-interest took over. In fact, the company was
right—most of the employees would not be with the company
long enough for their pensions to vest, so the company's proposal wasn't all that expensive from their perspective. It was a
good example of breaking down theory into reality. The members of the negotiating committee were able to dispense with the*

theory and look instead at a sheet of paper listing their expected earnings under the company plan. And it looked pretty good to them. They ended up accepting the company proposal. Still, had the company kept insisting that (a) this was not a very big issue and (b) the deal would ratify even without this provision, they'd probably still be sitting there, arguing. Understand your counterparts and their various interests.

Here are a few more brief illustrations of the principle that issues and interests have names and stories behind them. Relatively minor issues are made larger by the fact that they have a direct effect on the negotiating committee or your counterpart. If you can identify the interests behind the interests, you can address them more easily and more directly. And, in most of these cases, one side's ability to address these relatively inexpensive issues directly impacted the other side's willingness to deal on other issues.

The "B-Scale" is a phenomenon born in the airline industry in the eighties. It was a new—and lower—pay scale for newly hired people. That is, existing employees would be on the A-scale, which might have eight or ten steps (i.e., your pay moves up to the next step every year on your anniversary date). The B-scale was shorter, and the levels of pay at each step were lower. Once you reached the top of the B-scale, you would then merge into the A-scale. When parties sat down to negotiate, they would negotiate the levels of pay on both scales, and the union would press to make the B-scale as short as possible.

As in the pension example above, typically the union negotiating committee is made up of senior people, and thus it is rare that there are any B-scalers present. However, in one case, a very seasoned union negotiator had just joined the airline from one of the many airlines that had gone out of business in the aftermath of deregulation. He was the lead negotiator, but since he was new with this company, he was being paid on the B-scale. I've never seen a negotiating committee fight so hard over the B-scale, but this was no theoretical argument. The new man was watching that scale very carefully, and no deal was going to be put out to the membership for ratification until he was satisfied with the level and the duration of the B-scale. It was an odd twist, in that the company wasn't used to paying this much attention to the issue, but in this case, they were absolutely required to address it to his satisfaction.

In a similar case, the company in negotiations was actually the product of three different companies, which had merged over the previous few years since the last agreement had been negotiated. One of the big, overriding issues was the rationalization of three different labor agreements into one. As you might imagine, they all had different levels of benefits. One of the companies had a particularly lean pension plan from the employees' perspective. One of the members of the small negotiating team was from that company and was determined to improve the pension for himself and his former colleagues. Once again, it would have otherwise been one small issue, impacting only a small part of the company. However, because this one employee sat on the negotiating committee, the company spent much more time and money on the issue—and on making those employees whole—than they anticipated.

One last vignette, illustrating a variation of the same point (i.e., the negotiating committee members' own interests and their impact on a particular negotiation). I was working on a case involving a fairly small group of employees, yet the union negotiating committee consisted of eighteen people. It was a nightmare—as much for the union's lead negotiator as it was for the company or for me. They had been negotiating for most of the year and time had long since passed when they should be down to a few issues, yet a hundred or more remained. We weren't making much progress and I asked the top union negotiator to try to come up with a list of "gottas," a list of the things he really needed out of this negotiation. I wasn't going to give it to the company. It was for my own edification and it was an exercise meant to focus their minds as well. I expected a list of no more than a half dozen items. When he came back to me later in the day, sure enough, he had his list—of eighteen items. When we looked down the list together, I could almost put the name of the person on the negotiating committee next to their corresponding "pet" issue. Many were very minor, but we went to work with the company to address them. As we made our way through each person's issue, the end—the deal—grew nearer at last. Issues and interests have names and stories behind them.

One final point on the above negotiation, offered as much for comic relief as for its educational value: We finally reached a deal a week or two later, but for the last session we sat in a room, just the company negotiator, the union negotiator, and I. One of the issues in the original company proposal was to winnow the size of the union negotiating committee. The company paid them for their time and expenses while they were off negotiating—and in this negotiation that had been a considerable block of time. The costs were becoming prohibitive from the company's standpoint, and they wanted the union to have a negotiating committee more commensurate in size with the small group they represented. In that closing session, as all the big issues were initialed, the company remembered this last issue and raised it with the union negotiator.

"You really have to do something about the size of that committee," the company scolded, expecting a battle. "Eighteen people are just way too many to represent a group this size!" Their ire seemed to grow with each word. "We propose that you *shrink the committee at least down to ten!" they demanded.*

The union negotiator looked at the company negotiator, and spoke, totally beleaguered. "How about eight?"

We all laughed at the irony, and it broke all the tension, but he was as tired of dealing with eighteen different personalities as either the company or I was. He happily reduced the size of the committee, even beyond the level sought by the company. They had an easier negotiation the next time as a result.

A Special Rule Concerning Lawyers: Interests have layers and interests have lawyers. No discussion of layers of interests would be complete without some recognition of our friends at bar. If you ever have occasion to sell a house, there is a point in time where you begin to wonder for whom the realtor is working. He is supposed to be working for you, but you wonder. Like us, a realtor becomes wed to certain positions and ultimately just wants to make a deal, any deal. So, too, with lawyers, except they typically bill by the hour.

Every mediator who has been in the game long enough has seen lawyers get in the way of settlement. They no doubt have their sound professional reasons, but their advice and counsel often come out looking like shameless self-interest. If you are a party who is represented by a lawyer, you must ask yourself as you move through the process, "who has a stake in peace and who has a stake in war?" If your lawyer always seems to be talking you out of settling, beware. At some point, you must follow your instincts—your gut—and just sit down with your counterpart and make a deal. An unlikely source of wisdom: Wayne Newton, the Las Vegas entertainer, stumbled upon hard financial times some years ago. He went for advice to his friend Donald Trump, who had experienced a similar downturn years before. Trump's advice was to "get the lawyers out of it," to go see his creditors, talk directly to them, and work out a deal. Newton followed the advice, and soon he was on his way to financial recovery.

In the only case in which I have been involved as a defendant (see "Don't Negotiate, Mediate," chapter 5), my firm was being sued by our landlord for breaking our lease. We had had a very good and amicable relationship with our landlord up until that time. Once the lawsuit was filed, I wanted to reach out and call the landlord and work it out. I'm a lawyer by trade, but we deferred to our real estate lawyer, who continually advised us that this would be a huge mistake. In fact, two different lawyers gave us the same advice, even though my gut told me that there was nothing we couldn't fix face-to-face with the landlord. As recounted later in this book, by the time we went to court-ordered mediation, the firm's assets were depleted and there was no money left to pay the lawyers. It was at that point that we took control and moved to settlement by talking to the landlord face-to-face, as we knew we should have done all along.

There are many good lawyers out there who are dispensing good and sound advice. You should heed their advice. This section isn't intended to make the lawyers howl, although it most certainly will. It is cited here only to raise the issue that when you are the client, look for the economic interests around the table and weigh all advice accordingly.

The largest civil case in which I was ever involved as a mediator was a wrongful discharge suit against a large public university. There were a number of defendants, claiming a total of $21 million in damages. Some salient facts: Up until this point, this case had received almost no press attention. There were a number of defendants, many of them very sympathetic, including one stroke victim who was summarily fired after suffering his stroke, in spite of his more than twenty years of ser-

vice. *I spoke to each plaintiff individually. Some would have made terrific witnesses. A number of the female plaintiffs, in addition to their wrongful discharge suit, had filed sexual harassment claims against some very senior members of the school's administration during their employment. Their stories matched and, if they saw the light of day, would have been terribly embarrassing and moreover would have hurt the university's funding substantially.*

I'll fast-forward to the final conference I had with the parties. We had gone back and forth enough and the parties were now willing to settle for about a million dollars, in total. But the university's (outside) lawyer was completely intransigent. He was a litigator, a carnivore. He would not be moved and insisted that his client would not pay a cent to settle what he considered to be baseless charges. The days we spent interviewing the plaintiffs told me the charges were hardly baseless. Yet the lawyer told me he would continue to litigate this case until he found a judge who would agree with him. His clients sat in the room with him while he spoke. I made all the arguments to him when I caucused alone with the university: the chances of losing a $21 million lawsuit; the public embarrassment of some of the revelations of the discharges; the personal and public humiliation of the people who were accused of sexual harassment, who were still very much in the university's leadership; and the damage to the university's ability to raise money from alumni and the community. Still he was not phased. I asked the university how much it had cost them thus far to defend themselves. "About a million dollars" came the reply. I asked the lawyer how much he thought it would cost them to continue through the lawsuit. "About another million," he replied matter-of-factly. If they lost the lawsuit it would cost them more, either to pay the verdict or to appeal. A million dollars was the lowest dollar *amount they would spend. I tried to reason with the client that about $900,000 that day would get them out of there scot-free and put this ugly episode behind them. The university representative squirmed in his chair. He kept saying he agreed with me, that it all made perfect sense to him but that his lawyer was quite adamant about not letting them settle. Adamant indeed.*

In my view, this was a lawyer who put his own economic interests—and his interest in continued legal sparring over arcane legal issues—over the clear economic and reputational and public interests of his client.

Almost all lawyers are good, decent, honest, God-fearing people, who will give you good, sound advice. However, if your lawyer continually tells you not to mediate, not to settle, not to talk to your counterpart, beware, especially if his advice runs counter to what common sense and your own best instincts tell you. Recall the lawyers in this chapter, who represented other companies in the queue who would be negotiating with the same union. They had their own views, their own positions, and their own fish to fry, all at this particular client's expense.

When all else fails, as Donald Trump advised, "Get the lawyers out."

Clearly Define the Interest: This is a subset or a clarification of the two previous points. First, you need to be aware of the layers of interests around the table. Next, you should figure out whose interest is driving a particular issue. Finally you need to clearly define the interest. Most of the time, the interest is clear, but not always. You can make a mistaken assumption about what the true issue is and waste time and energy trying to address it, but in reality be far from the mark.

I was helping a friend, a single mom, negotiate the purchase of her house in a new development. I fancied myself the negotia-

tor extraordinaire and figured I'd have an easy time moving the builder down on price. It was a new and fairly affluent neighborhood, but there were only a few homes left. They were cookiecutters of a sort, all very similar, but they were distinguished by their amenities—deck, sunroom, finished basement, and so on.

I sat down with the builder and found he was absolutely intractable on price. I couldn't believe it. I literally couldn't move him a dime off a several hundred thousand-dollar price. I tried every trick in the book but he would not be moved.

Finally, it hit me: his interest was in keeping up his "comps" (i.e., the comparable prices of all the homes). He still had a few to sell, and he wanted to make sure they would all sell for the same price, to keep up the value of all the homes in the neighborhood. It took me a long time to realize this—longer than it should have, frankly. However, once I did, I was liberated. I just had to change my frame of reference. I went back to the builder. I asked him if, in return for her paying his asking price, would he be willing to put on a deck for her? "Sure," he said in an instant. How about a washer and dryer? "No problem." I was on a roll. A finished basement? "Yeah—we'll do that," he replied easily. It dawned on me that his interest wasn't just in getting rid of this house, in selling it on any terms. His interest was in selling it for this price, to maintain the "comparables," to hold the real estate values in place. If someone would agree to meet his interest (i.e., pay his price), he was more than willing to be accommodating on the amenities. That is, you must pay the price, but you sure could negotiate like crazy on the amenities, and she did. So much so, in fact, that she gained far more options and add-ons for her house than we did with our own, which we had bought years before. I learned an interesting lesson that day about being very sure about what the issue is that you're trying to address before you actually try to address it.

Be clear about whose interest you're addressing and be absolutely certain about what that interest is before you start throwing money or solutions at it. This is not always easy and may take some probing, but don't just assume that you know what the interest is.

Credibility Counts: As in life, credibility counts in negotiations. In fact, your only stock in trade is your word. Negotiators hurt their credibility in two main ways: by making promises they don't keep and making threats that they don't keep. On promises, it's a relatively simple proposition. If you promise your counterpart you'll do something (often in exchange for a concession from them), then do it. Most people keep their word, but if you don't, you'll be damaged for the remainder of the negotiation. If you promise a quid for a quo, deliver.

As for "threats," a loose term, the most predominant way parties hurt their credibility is by setting artificial deadlines. Negotiations—especially those involving many issues—are very tedious. Every now and then the public gets a glimpse of a high-profile negotiation at the eleventh hour. The excitement, the tension, the drama are palpable. Yet this is like judging all political campaigns by election night. Not evident are the days and months of whiling away the hours in hotel rooms and at Rotary Club meetings. So, too, with negotiation. At least 99 percent of it is pretty tedious. As a result, parties—even the most seasoned ones—can grow quite frustrated with the pace of negotiations. They grow frustrated that their counterpart is not accepting their offer promptly enough. To get things moving, parties will often attempt to set an artificial deadline (i.e., "You have until tomorrow to accept this deal"). The correct question is, "Or else *what?*" The moving party might say, "Or else we're selling that particular business unit," or the completely asinine, "Because it will be off the table after that date." Let's examine the former excuse first. Hard deadlines are indeed very rare. If indeed there's some reason that you must sell that business on that precise day, then do it. However, the chances are that your counterpart won't believe your deadline any more than you believe it upon reading it here. In all probability, you can't take a step that big in a short period of time. And, right up until the actual time of sale—no doubt months hence—it can be reversed. If this is an idle threat, it will be viewed as such and you'll never be able to set another deadline.

As for taking things off the table, it can't be done. (See "Rules," chapter 5). Suffice it to say that once your counterparts have seen what you're willing to do—even if it's by date certain—you've re-set the floor from which all negotiations will proceed from that moment forward. Saying they'd better accept it or it will disappear is specious. No one buys that, either, and it hurts your credibility. Don't do it unless the deadline is real (the first one in history), then stick to it.

You may recall that in the baseball strike in the early nineties, where several mediators were involved. Finally, the president himself became involved and summoned the parties to the White House. He told them they must accept the deal he proposed by a date certain. When that date came and went with no action by either side, he moved the date a few days forward. When that day came and went, he moved it again.

Truth is, any one of these arbitrary deadlines after the first one is completely meaningless. Once you miss your first one, your credibility is gone. You become the negotiator who cried "Wolf." Your counterpart will never believe another deadline from you.

Don't make promises or "threats"—like setting deadlines— that you don't intend to keep.

Don't Get Caught Up in "Shape of the Table" Issues: You may recall that in the Paris Peace Talks aimed at ending the Vietnam War, the parties argued for months over the proper shape of the table, at which sat representatives from many countries and factions. This lore has worked its way into negotiating parlance. When parties are arguing over preliminary, atmospheric, nonsubstantive issues, it is said that they are debating the shape of the table. Parties are everlastingly attaching preconditions to their negotiations. They can also be viewed as "love tests," one party's effort to test the other party's depth of commitment to getting a deal.

Party A will meet only in Cleveland. Party B will meet only in Chicago, and never Cleveland, but maybe St. Louis. Party A will come only if Party B doesn't bring the obnoxious man in the brown hat. Party A will meet only during the first half of the month, Party B only during the second half. Party A wants Party B to make the first proposal, Party B wants Party A to go first.

Negotiations are hard enough without borrowing all of this ancillary trouble. You should not do it unless you're trying to delay the negotiation, a legitimate tactic. However, assuming you are interested in reaching a prompt agreement, you ought not attach any preconditions. What do you do if they're used against you? As a mediator, it's well nigh impossible to fix them, since both parties can be intractable and have their own negotiation-within-a-negotiation. As a negotiator, the answer is simple: You should give in. That's right, give in. "But won't I look weak?!?" you ask. Forget it. Let's assume you've done your homework, and you have a clear idea of your principles and your priorities. Unless the issue violates one of your principles or is on your list of priorities, let it go. In most cases, once you've called your counterpart's bluff, it doesn't seem that important to meet in Cleveland after all. Once you've proven your love, that you're willing to address their minor (if petty) concerns, these concerns evaporate. Some might say that there are more where that came from and you ought not run yourself ragged, but in the first few instances, call their bluff and meet wherever, whenever, on whatever condition they want. What do you care? There will be plenty of time to "look tough" once the negotiations begin.

As important as this rule is, it is meaningless without its corollary:

Pick Up the Points for Making Concessions: If this is a negotiation-within-a-negotiation, then you must act accordingly. Once you arrive in Cleveland, make it clear to your counterpart that you are there because apparently meeting there was important to them. You saw its importance (since they were so insistent) and in the interest of getting an agreement, you decided to meet them in Cleveland. "In the interest of getting an agreement." Paste those words in your wallet, inside the visor of your hat, inside your briefcase. Use them like a mantra. "In the interest of getting an agreement," you are here in Cleveland, you will meet when you otherwise weren't available, you will not bring the obnoxious guy in the brown hat, whatever. All in the interest of getting an agreement. Your goal is to drain the swamp. Everything you do—all movement, all concessions—must move you toward that goal, or don't do it. The following is an example of a negotiator who was the worst of both worlds, violating both of the previous tenets.

This was a lengthy negotiation between a mid-sized company and its largest union. In this particular case, the union's main interest was in dragging out the proceedings. The company's interest was in concluding a swift deal. For the moment, the union seemed to have the upper hand.

The chief negotiator for the company was completely hung up on being right in all instances, on every proposal. The union negotiator was very skilled and tied the company negotiator in knots over and over again. As a mediator, to some degree I had to leave the parties to their own devices, while still trying to move the process along.

One day I sat in combination disbelief and abject boredom as the parties argued over one word—a single word—for most of the day. It wasn't a particularly important word, either. But, it was the company's word, and by God, they were going to get it in the agreement. The union was playing the company negotiator like a piano. They just kept arguing for the primacy of their word over the company's word, knowing full well that the company would never relent and the union would achieve their goal of delay. Finally, my eyes rolling back in my head, I couldn't stand it for one more second. I called a recess, and called the company negotiator into a side room and closed the door.

"You're doing great in there," I said.

"Really?" he said, smiling.

"Yes," I replied. "I had no idea how important this word was to you, but now I know. You are doing a fantastic job of making the case for this one word," I continued. "Now, I just assume that when we get to other issues, like wages, pensions, and health care, that they'll just fall into place, since you're apparently using all your energy on this word."

I made my point, and he grew sheepish. If he was going to spend most of one day arguing over one word, where were his priorities? What would he do when we moved to important issues? Worse still, he was playing completely into the union's hands on delay when he had the opposite interest. He was so caught up in being right that he had lost sight of his priorities and his central goal of concluding a swift agreement. At the rate he was going, he would not conclude an agreement in his lifetime.

I opened the door and he walked dejectedly back into the room as the parties were starting to reconvene. But he was the worst of both worlds in this important respect: Apparently deciding that he was ultimately going to have to compromise on this word, he just walked back into the room and said, "Let's go on to something else," and they did. The next day, when the company passed a hundred-plus-page proposal across the table to the union, he had relented, had accepted their word. It was buried in the proposal and I don't think anyone saw it or noticed it. He compromised on the issue and he didn't pick up any points for doing so.

Our company negotiator in the example above—having decided to give in on his word—should have walked back in the room and said, "Upon further reflection, I'll accept your word in this agreement. I still think my word is OK, but *in the interest of reaching an agreement,* I'll compromise so we can move on to the next issue." He should acknowledge that this issue appears important to them, and in the interest of accommodating them, of initialing one more item, of moving one step closer to reaching an agreement, he will give in. Instead, he committed one of the gravest sins of negotiation: he gave in and gained nothing from it.

Verify "Awfulisms": This is a new and creative term that has crept its way into the negotiation lexicon. "Awfulisms" are scenarios that show the implications of a proposal in the extreme. They are typically rhetorical and hysterical and are intended to show the proposal in a light in which it was never intended to be and indeed in which it will never be realized. Awfulisms are usually intended, of course, to defeat the proposal at which they are aimed. If they are used against you by your counterpart, you must recognize them for what they are and debunk them immediately and rationally.

This case involved a small regional airline, which flew among several Middle Atlantic States. On the table was a proposal from the company, which spelled out when pilots would be on reserve (or stand-by) and when they would be required to work. It aimed to require some pilots to be on call during the day, so the company could call them into service if needed.

The union, however, objected loudly. In their view, under the company's proposal, a pilot could be required to be available and "on call" for up to twelve hours. What if, they asked, the company called the pilot into work a minute before his or her twelve-hour reserve period expired? They would then begin their work day, which could potentially (under the contract) run another eight to ten hours. All told, went the argument, these pilots could be without rest for twenty hours or more. The union argued that this would certainly put them in violation of the spirit—if not the letter—of Federal Aviation Administration (FAA) regulations.

I believe in this particular case the argument was earnest, and the company certainly engaged the union in discussion and sometimes heated debate. The parties argued back and forth about how this proposal would work, and how they might prevent someone from working a twenty-hour day. Since I had the benefit of being the mediator, I was able to take a step back from the discussion. At some point, it occurred to me that this was a regional airline. I interrupted the parties.

"Excuse me," I said, "But when does the last flight in your system land each day?"

"Our last flight for the day?" asked the company. They thought for a minute. "Well, let's see, it arrives at X location at about

9:30 P.M." The union nodded its assent. They mentioned, too, that this was a bit of an aberration, and that most of the flying was done an hour or more before then.

I continued, "And what time does your first flight in the system leave in the morning each day?"

"The first flight out" (also about an hour earlier than most, they told me), "is around 7:30 A.M." This meant that the entire airline was in operation for only about fourteen hours each day. They all sat for a moment and pondered the implications. Since they did no flying from roughly 9:30 P.M. until 7:30 A.M., there was really no way that anyone would be expected to work beyond those hours. Thus, the entire prior discussion was moot. However, had it not been called to their attention, they would have continued to debate it, and may well have put language in the contract that would have addressed the "awfulism." It would have burned much needed energy and time and would have squandered political and negotiating capital. By moving from the awfulism to the specific, we were for the moment saved.

In some instances, parties intentionally use awfulisms to advance their point of view. You must be vigilant to your counterpart's attempts to characterize your proposal or theirs in a way that defies reality.

The issue, once again, was health care. This particular company was having a problem as the biggest employer in the area. Their health-care plan was quite generous, and the employee share of premiums was quite low. Their problem was that everyone wanted to have their health care through this particular employer. Given the chance, every two-earner couple, every family opted for their coverage over that provided by the other spouse's company. The company was talking to the union about ways to keep more unwanted people out of their system to avoid driving up costs. The union was not terribly sympathetic at first blush.

The company pressed its case. They said they had a litany of people whose use of the system bordered on abuse. In fact, they said, there was one employee who somehow managed to remain on some extended leave of absence for a year, but kept some undefined connection to the company just to maintain her health-care benefits for her and her family. In fact, the company said (incredibly), she never even set foot on company property for that entire year, yet remained insured under the company plan.

The union negotiator was well-seasoned and very low-key. He listened intently to the company's tale of woe. When they finished, he spoke.

"Now, Bob," he said in his slow monotone, addressing the company negotiator, "Would that be the exception" he paused for effect, "or the rule?" It made everyone laugh, but he also made his point. True, the company had a problem, but the example they used was a bit ridiculous. It persuaded no one. Later, by talking more realistically about the problems in the middle of the curve and not at the margins, they were able to reach agreement.

Avoid using awfulisms—they hurt your credibility. Aim for the middle. Solve those problems. Don't worry about those at the margins. And if your counterpart uses awfulisms against you, meet them and shine the light of logic on them. Let your counterpart know you are willing to address the problems that are most prevalent, but also let them know that you are unwilling to spend your time on aberrations. Move it from bizarre and comic theory to calm and rational practice. Once that is done, the issue can be solved.

Make Realistic Proposals: This may seem obvious, but years of practice reveal that it is not. In fact, quite the opposite. Too often, people take an overly simplistic view of negotiations.

Many, if not most, people believe that negotiations are at core about "splitting the difference," plain and simple. Thus, if you seek a 5 percent pay raise, you ask for 10 percent. A company that is willing to give a 3 percent raise might as a result offer nothing. Someone who's ready to pay $40,000 for a car might walk on the lot and offer $30,000, based on nothing. A person seeking a 10 percent raise from their boss goes in to ask for 20 percent to leave themselves "some room to negotiate." These are all real and practical examples of how most people approach negotiations. Yet, in fact, negotiations are a complex process, involving many issues both substantive and "atmospheric," like ego and power and leverage. If it were as simple as asking for twice what you really wanted, you'd not need negotiators or mediators, only a good calculator.

Parties also tend to "negotiate" through the sheer bulk of their proposals, too. Often, a party will cloak a weak proposal in dozens of other proposals, hoping to use up their counterpart's good will—and their ability to say no—on ancillary issues, so they can gain what they want on their big issue. But negotiations don't work that way. You should not feel constrained in your ability to say "no." It is limitless. Sometimes, your counterparts need to hear it, so they are clear about where you stand and what you are able to do. Like the vignette in chapter 4, parties who hear "maybe" or "just a little" will keep coming back for more. Sometimes you need to just say no, with no apologies necessary.

Both these approaches—aiming too high (on purpose) and burying your counterpart with proposals—are dangerous. They are dangerous not only because they overstate the gap between the parties, but in so doing, they sap hope and damage the relationship. It is very easy for the person on the other side of outrageous proposals to grow discouraged, because the gulf appears much too wide to bridge. It also instills great anger and frustration and thus damages the relationship between you and your counterpart, sometimes just as you're getting started, as you're getting a peek for the first time into their minds, via their proposal. In labor negotiations, as in other more public disputes, parties use their counterparts' outrageous opening positions to coalesce and to foment ire on their own side or with the public. Don't unintentionally give ammunition to your counterpart by making proposals that overreach, just because you think you're giving yourself lots of room to negotiate. You're not—you're digging yourself a hole. Recall the earlier discussion on face-saving. The more outrageous your proposals, the harder it will be for you to save face. Don't make this process any harder than it already is.

There are some negotiations where one party is trying to anger or aggravate the other. If that's the case, then make your proposals as outrageous as you'd like. Just don't expect to get a deal soon. However, if your goal is to conclude a deal in a timely and amicable way, avoid these traps.

The goal is to make proposals that give your counterparts a difficult decision. You need not take particular delight in it, but to the extent you make them squirm, your proposal is right where it should be. It's too easy for a salesman to reject your $30,000 offer on a $40,000 car. It's harder for them to reject a $39,000 offer on the same car. In fact, it may be easy for them to accept it and if they accept too quickly, you aimed too high. Perhaps the right number is $37,000 or $38,000, depending on what your homework, your research reveals. You want to make an offer that really makes them have to stretch to meet you. That's the ideal proposal, one that's not accepted too quickly or rejected too quickly. And, remember, when you're the seller, you can move in only one direction on price, that is, down.

The best example of this comes from the perspective of the mediator, not the negotiator.

I was mediating a civil case one day in small claims court. It was a personal injury case where the plaintiff, the injured party was seeking $5,500. Unfortunately, the facts were against him in that two eyewitnesses said he ran a red light, and his treating physician had since died, and thus was not available to testify on his behalf.

At the outset, the insurance company offered—through me— $500. After some prodding, they said they could go to $750, but in no case could they—would they—ever go "to four figures." I then met with the plaintiff and told him it looked like the insurance company would go only for "minimal value." He asked, "What about $2,200?" I told him I just didn't see it. I didn't want to defeat him, to sap his hope, his willingness to try, by telling him what the company said (i.e., that they couldn't go to "four figures"). I couched it instead in terms of "minimal value." He asked, "What about a thousand?" I told him I didn't know. He said he'd settle for $1,000.

I walked back into the room where the insurance company was and told them "we can all go home" for a thousand dollars. The insurance company representative had to call to get authorization for anything over $750. Before she called, I told her that if they could agree to $1,000, I wouldn't be coming back to them for more (e.g., $1,250). That is, if she could get the $1,000, that would settle this (very weak) case.

Sure enough, she received authorization for $1,000. Had I asked her for $1,500, it would most certainly have been a "hell, no."

The $1,000 number in the above instance was in the range between what they could accept and what they simply could not abide. It was an unimportant small case and a narrow range, to be sure, but the lesson is clear. You must aim your proposals for that same magic band between what they can accept and what they can all too easily reject out of hand. Do your homework, and make your proposals accordingly.

Beware of "The Rock": This notion logically follows the one just presented, in that it pertains to which party has the difficult decision, or "the rock" on them. In the absence of difficult decisions, negotiations are easy. They become very difficult when you have to stretch to reach your counterpart's proposal, to make a significant move in his direction, or to accept some measure of something you're not terribly willing to accept. As long as your counterpart makes outrageous proposals, you will never know the rock. It will never rest on you. Similarly, if you make outrageous and unreachable proposals, your counterpart will never know the glory of being under the rock, either. Your job as a negotiator—part of your mission to gain an agreement, to reach a deal—is to put your counterpart under the rock as much as you can. Simply put, it's shifting the tough decision—the rock—to your counterpart.

In the early days of any negotiation, when there are dozens or hundreds of items, there really is no rock, or at least it doesn't rest on anyone. However, when you begin to approach a negotiation's end, the rock will emerge quite clearly and will begin to move back and forth between the parties. Like the children's game of "hot potato," the name of the game is to get it off of you and onto your counterpart as quickly and as often as possible.

In the closing hours of one negotiation, I had only the two principal—and very skilled—negotiators in the room with me, and they were trying to solve the only two issues that remained, issue X and issue Y. Not surprisingly, they were both significant issues. It was fascinating to watch these two, like masters, move the rock back and forth, using the old reliable "what if." For most of the discussion, I was a mere spectator.

The union negotiator would say, "If I give you what you want on issue X, will you give me what I want on issue Y?" That would put the rock on the company negotiator, and give him a tough decision to make. He would ponder for a moment and toss it back on the union negotiator.

"If I give you what you want on issue X, will you give me what I want on issue Y?" That put the union negotiator under the rock, with a very tough decision to make.

Finally, the company negotiator needed to consult the CEO. He told his counterpart that he couldn't go to his CEO with a hypothetical. The union negotiator was going to have to give him a concrete proposal. The union negotiator thus dropped the "what if" and flat out offered issue X in return for issue Y. I turned to the company negotiator, shrugged, and said, "No more hypothetical." He nodded and stepped into the next room to call— and put the big rock on—the CEO. The CEO capitulated and we had our deal, but watching that rock move back and forth in the closing minutes was as fascinating a process as I've ever seen. I don't think anyone held it for longer than a few minutes. Each was trying to push the tough decision off on his counterpart. Ultimately, the deal was done.

Brainstorm: It is *your* job—not your counterpart's—to find a solution. All too often, negotiators become too bogged down in the give-and-take of the negotiation process. They push paper back and forth at one another and when problems arise, they stop and don't know what to do. There will be more on this later (see "Negotiation is 50 percent Sales, 50 percent Psychology" and "Don't Negotiate, Mediate," both in chapter 5), but it is important to note here that you can't leave the problem-solving to your counterpart or in all likelihood it won't get done.

When you hit an apparent impasse, it is your job to brainstorm. Think of any and all possible solutions. The nitty-gritty of negotiations is two-dimensional. You must make them three-dimensional and try to see solutions where none are obvious. The typical person, typical negotiator, accepts the given boundaries and takes "no" for an answer. You must use your creativity to test the parameters, to push the envelope, and to try to see your way clear to an agreement.

Chapter 5

Rules

The previous chapter focused on steering you through a particular negotiation. This chapter will focus on some overarching rules that cover all negotiations and that are almost always true. They have been distilled from hundreds of disputes and are lessons which are common to all.

Negotiations Are As Much About the Process As About the Substance: This probably goes without saying in light of all that has gone before, but it will be stated here nonetheless. The process includes all the issues covered above, such as the many "atmospherics," like the tone of the negotiation, issues of ego and respect, the many "love tests" you face, and so forth. Negotiations are often time consuming because they are the process of getting people in the right frame of mind to compromise. As noted above, negotiations are about so much more than simply splitting the difference. Were it that easy, we would only need computers and mathematicians, not negotiators and mediators.

In the first case in which I was ever involved as a federal mediator, my newcomer's impatience had made me restless, and so I drafted a "mediator's proposal" to move the parties off of their inertia and toward a deal. Suffice it to say the results were disastrous (See "Mediators: Lessons and Observations," chapter 6). Weeks later when they finally reached their deal, I took my mediator's proposal (which I had saved) to one of the most senior mediators in the organization. He had advised me strongly against making the proposal in the first place, but I stupidly ignored his advice. Now that the deal had been reached, I wanted him to see how close my mediator's proposal was to the actual final deal. He looked at it and just smiled. He put his arm on my shoulder and said, "We always know about where they're going to end up," he said, "The trick is getting them there."

Another scenario illustrates the same point and a miscalculation made as a result of a wrong assumption.

I had been working on a multi-party case involving three different organizations. One organization was the prime mover, however, and had been pushing the other two organizations— and me—to get an agreement. One of the top executives from that organization had been diligent in talking to the other two and in keeping me briefed fully on the latest developments. One day, he talked to me about what he thought the other parties could accept. It sounded completely logical to me. In fact, as it turns out, he had been having conversations with both groups, and he believed this solution was acceptable to them.

"Why haven't you proposed this to them?" I asked.

"Because," he answered, "this is such an obvious solution,

the fact that they haven't yet done it tells me that I must be wrong."

I had to laugh at the irony of it all. In fact, his was a completely logical assumption. However, I reminded him of all the political fighting and personal enmity between those two groups. I told him there was so much baggage between the heads of the two groups that it was unlikely they could ever see their way clear to a deal, obvious or not. What was keeping them apart was not the substance. There were so many "atmospherics" that they couldn't see their way clear to the substance on their best day. Truth was, he was probably going to have to hit them over the head with the solution before they'd ever realize it. They were too busy fighting.

There is clearly much substance to be finessed and resolved in any negotiation. However, there are infinitely more process types of issues surrounding every negotiation. In some ways, they are the more important. They keep people apart, and you ignore them at your peril. As a negotiator, you must be of a mind to compromise and you must bring your counterpart around to the same mindset. Picking the mid-point is easy. Getting there is hard.

Be Patient: Negotiations are full of ups and downs. False hope and false despair are the twin-headed Hydra of dispute resolution. The best negotiators and the best mediators have the patience of Job. Patience is the passive side of persistence. You need both skills—patience and persistence—to endure and to succeed as a negotiator. Remember that most negotiations are a marathon, not a sprint. As mentioned above, you build the relationship as you go. You can take as many strokes as necessary to complete the task. Impatience is a virus that will lead you to try to force a solution before your counterpart is ready. Precisely because negotiations are about process, you must bide your time and wait for your counterpart to be ready to compromise. Forcing the issue will almost always backfire.

Everything Is Negotiable: This is one of the most reliable rules not only in negotiations but also in life. Once you learn to ask questions and push the envelope, things that appeared immutable to you become eminently moveable. Once you begin to look at life through a negotiator's eyes, you stop accepting existing parameters and boundaries and start asking "Why?" When you do, the incredible randomness of life becomes terribly apparent. Beware, however: Negotiating can become an obsession.

In labor negotiations, parties exchange opening proposals and under applicable law, a party is not required to negotiate over anything that was not in the other side's proposal. However, for the right price, anything can work its way into a negotiation. In fact, a shrewd negotiator will extract a price for even agreeing to discuss the issue and hopefully some concessions for settling the substance of the issue itself.

However, the more interesting application of this mischievous rule is in the layperson's marketplace: buying a car, a suit, a meal, negotiating a lease, you name it. All aspects of every deal are really open for discussion. In truth, people seldom push the envelope. There are, however, two caveats: use common sense, and make sure you're dealing with someone who has the authority to make a deal. Don't try to negotiate the toll on the Golden Gate Bridge. You'll be arrested. Don't try to get the kid at the fast food counter to throw in an extra cheeseburger. He doesn't have the authority. There's no button for that on the cash register. Don't ask a bank teller to throw in an extra few dollars. She'll go to jail. Use your head.

Assuming you are not dealing with the far end of the spectrum (i.e., with an item that is truly not negotiable) and assuming you are dealing with someone who has the authority to move on price, just remember to ask one central question. Once they quote you a price, just ask, "Can you do any better?"

This is offered as a gift to you. These five words will more than pay for the cost of this book, and if you use it correctly and frequently, will pay for your investment in this book many times over. It is so simple, but it almost always triggers a positive response. And, almost no one asks the question. You will be astounded at its effectiveness.

A friend had only recently made the decision that he needed a new car. He had done no homework, no research. He had only the vaguest idea of what price range he was in and had no idea what model he wanted. He had much work ahead of him, but decided to start on a date certain.

On that day, he decided to eat lunch at his desk. He opened up the local paper and turned to the ads for the automotive dealerships. He wondered first and foremost how much this would cost him in terms of financing. He dialed the number that appeared in the largest print on the page, and was immediately transferred to an eager salesman.

"Hi," said my friend, "Can you tell me what your interest rate is?"

"Seven and a half percent" came the confident reply.

My friend hesitated only a moment. "Can you do any better?"

Replied the voice on the phone, "Six point nine."

The above vignette, almost comical, illustrates the point. The person in this scenario had done absolutely no homework yet, but already had shaved over a half point off his interest rate just by asking the question.

My wife was calling hotels in Jackson, Wyoming, a few months in advance of our planned summer vacation. "What's your best rate?" she asked the first place she called.

"Two hundred and twenty dollars a night," they answered. She, of course, pressed. "Can you do any better?"

"One seventy-nine," came the reply.

Not to pick on hotels, but the final vignette also happened at the check-in desk:

I was checking into a hotel where I had a reservation and the clerk very dutifully pulled up the applicable record on the computer. A furrow crossed her brow. She looked across the counter at me, quizzically. "What rate did we quote you?" she asked.

I smiled. "The lowest one you've got," I answered, facetiously. I had no intention of revealing my rate until I heard hers. While she clicked away on the computer, I dug in my bag for the confirmation slip. We were like two poker players, both holding and looking at our own cards.

"What rate are you looking at on your screen?" I asked, "What's your corporate rate?" She said they actually had me booked at a rate ($175) lower than their corporate rate ($200). At that moment, I realized that I was there to speak to an annual meeting of a business group. I asked her what their rate was.

"One sixty," she answered.

"Good," I said, "I'll take it." Just by standing there, pushing the envelope a bit, negotiating on a rate most people simply accept, I was able to save $40 per night. I'm not any smarter than the average person, and I would never have done this before I began negotiating. Having seen what is possible allows me to push the envelope, to refuse to take the answer as given.

One final vignette, because it's fun:

My wife bought me in-line skates for Christmas a few years ago. Either through oversight or because she was hoping to collect on insurance money, she did not buy me any protective pads

for wrists, elbows, and knees. I went to the sporting goods fran-
chise at the local mall. Like my car-buying friend in the above
scenario, I had done no research and knew absolutely nothing
about how much it would cost.

"I need pads for in-line skating," I said to the salesperson.
He walked over to a large display and plucked off a package
with a complete set of pads. "Here," he said confidently, "Ev-
erything you need is in here." I looked at the price: $50. It struck
me as a little high, based on absolutely nothing. For all I knew,
the place across the mall could have been selling them for $10
or $100.

I stared at the price and expressed some surprise. "Fifty
bucks—wow!" I said. "Can you do any better?"

He looked at me for only an instant. "Forty," he said.

That was better.

Airlines have different rates. Hotels have different rates. So
do car dealers, all retailers, landlords, banks, and just about any
seller of goods, services, and information that you can imagine.
The trick is to negotiate the best rate, the best price you can for
whatever item you're buying.

There is a corollary question that you can also ask, which is,
"Have you sold this item for less?" Of course, this question
doesn't imply "since the dawn of civilization." Only ask if
they've recently sold it for less. You will be amazed at the response. People are by nature honest and indeed most salespeople
will be honest with you. You will be surprised how often the
item has just been on sale, or is just going on sale (you want to
ask if it *will* sell for less, too). You will find that there's a discount if you perform some meaningless act, like filling out a
survey or giving them your e-mail address. You'll find there are
discounts for people who belong to the same club that you belong to or for kids in your school. You will be absolutely aston-

ished. Salespeople will reveal to you that their big sale just ended or will begin tomorrow. There are all sorts of incentive programs out there from parent companies. Many retailers advertise that they will match the lowest price on any item. Even those who don't advertise it will often do it. Car dealers sell at a discount to certain buying clubs that are about as exclusive as joining the YMCA. Spend the $25 to join the buying club and save $500 on the car.

Negotiating really is a mindset—some would say a sickness—and you've been cautioned about its potential of becoming an obsession, especially when it's a new skill and you realize its power. We are a nation of laws and we are generally law abiding. We drive at the speed limit, we pay our taxes, and we tend to accept existing parameters. But vendors and sellers are not the United States Government. They're in business to sell, not to turn away sales. Again, if you live in an affluent area and are trying to buy the hot new luxury car, you're probably going to pay the sticker price or higher. But assuming that you're not buying an item that's in extreme demand, you can negotiate all sorts of better deals.

And, this doesn't apply only to buyers, it pertains to sellers, too. You can set your own parameters, even if they're outside the market, out of the ordinary.

A neighbor was selling his house in a wild seller's market. He was finally building his dream home and would be taking occupancy of it, but not for another eight months. He was worried about when to put his home on the market. Indeed, stories were legion of home sellers who sold the day the house went on the market, and some even before—literally. These houses were selling for the asking price and in some circumstances even beyond. He was wondering when to put his house on the market so he could coordinate it with his entry into the new home. The last thing he wanted to do was to have to move to temporary quarters for a short period of time and maybe put all his belongings in storage. He was asking my advice as to when he might want to put his house out there in this manic seller's market. Incidentally, he also asked me about what price he should ask for the house.

On his first question, my advice was for him to put it on the market now. He looked at me in panic. However, I told him he should be clear up front that he wouldn't be able to move out for some time. I know this probably violates every rule of real estate, but my view was to make his own terms, make his own contract, shape his own deal. In that market, he just might get his way. Furthermore everything is negotiable, and I explained to him that it cuts both ways. In the light most favorable to him, he can place any terms or caveats on the sale that he wishes. Anyone who falls in love with the house can try to move him off those terms, most likely with money.

On the other hand, if he received a really good offer, but the buyer needed to move in right away and didn't want to pay for the privilege, then he had a decision to make, that is, whether to sell then or to pass up this buyer and wait and hope for another. But certainly at that point, it would be a negotiating point for him to pursue. If worse came to worse, he could put his stuff in storage after all. In truth, as a negotiator, you can also see that this eight-month gap was not insurmountable if each side absorbs a piece of it. Time does pass, and home selling is time consuming. It just might be that if a buyer showed up on day one, he probably wouldn't be ready to move in immediately. If that's the case, then the seller has some time to play with, to get him closer to his dream house. If that (by some freak chance) were finished early, that eight months now starts to dwindle to a span of time that the two parties together can bridge by jiggling closing dates, for example, or arranging for a brief lease-back of the house. Part of negotiation is trying to make the insurmountable seem surmountable, and in this case it was.

On price, incidentally, I told him once he put a price on the house, he could only move one way. I urged him to put the price at the upper limit. Since he was in no hurry to sell, he had the luxury of time, to wait a few weeks to see whether anyone showed any interest in buying. If not, he could lower the price until the traffic picked up a bit. Better to do that, I said, than to price it lower and receive five offers the next day. That'll tell you that you priced it too low.

In short, everything—price, terms, timing, delivery, color, amenities, everything—is negotiable.

Nothing Is Ever "Off the Table": Let's change our frame of reference for a moment from the negotiating table to the courtroom. The prosecutor has just asked the defendant witness why, if he didn't commit the murder, did he in fact confess to it? The defense lawyer objects, and the judge bangs his gavel, reprimands the prosecutor, and sternly reminds him that the confession was inadmissible. He then turns to the jury to tell them to please disregard what they just heard (i.e., that the defendant in fact confessed to committing the crime). It is of course impossible to put the evidence back in the box. The jury heard it and will never forget it. It has been seared into their consciousness. In negotiations, it is similarly impossible to take an offer "off the table" and foolish to try.

Parties, however, seem to have a real passion for putting items on and taking items off the table. Sometimes they do it to move a recalcitrant counterpart (i.e., out of sheer petulance). Regardless of the reason, it is useless. Once that offer has seen the light of day, it is the new floor from which you negotiate.

We were nearing the strike deadline in one case and were meeting for a final week of negotiations in the hopes of averting a strike by week's end. Before we convened, the company sent a letter to all its employees who were represented by this union, making an offer. In it, they said the offer would be "pulled off the table" a few days before the strike deadline if their union negotiators didn't accept it. This of course had the effect of enraging the union and most of the employees, who saw it as a ham-handed effort by the company to control the negotiations. The company accomplished nothing except establishing a floor for the coming week of negotiations. The union knew that in no case could they come away with a deal worse than the one outlined in the company's letter to all employees.

The above tactic, of taking the offer "off the table" was asinine because, as in most cases, there was no magic event that would make this offer disappear. That is, there was no reversal of the company's economic condition—planned or unplanned—that would make this proposal inoperative on the day they were going to pull it off the table. Why couldn't the union accept it the next day or the day after? Because the company just didn't feel like giving as much that day? This is ridiculous. Once one party peeks at another party's cards, it becomes the floor from which all negotiations proceed. And, it has the additional effect of damaging a party's credibility—in this case the company's— by making a threat they couldn't enforce (see chapter 4, "Credibility Counts"). In short, don't put anything on the table if you don't intend to leave it there.

"Final" Doesn't Mean Final, "No" Doesn't Mean No: This rule, simply translated, means "context is everything." Words have no meaning without context, and this is no truer than in

negotiations. There is nothing like the sobriety caused by staring into the abyss to focus the mind.

Negotiators are everlastingly shopping "final" offers to the
other side. They're almost never final. If it's the twelfth hour
and you've been negotiating for a long time, maybe it will really be final, but it almost never is. Incredibly enough, in almost
every labor negotiation, the parties will push a document across
the table to their counterparts in the closing days or hours of a
negotiation and call it their "final, final, final" proposal. This is
comical, but true. It also makes one wonder whether it is 33
percent more final than the "final, final" offer that preceded it
or 66 percent more final than the "final" offer, which was conveyed first. It is as if saying the magic word, "final," three times,
will cast the proposal in stone and make it so. It doesn't. It only
saps your credibility (see chapter 4).

Just keep in mind that parties seem to have a genuine affec-
tion (or affliction) for terming their proposals "final" when
they're not. Don't be scared away by so-called final—or even
final, final, final—proposals. The final deal is the one that matters, the one to which you affix your signature. That's the only
one that counts.

"No" is even more prevalent. Think back to the poor fellow
in chapter 4 who screamed, "When are they going to get it—
that no means no?!?" They weren't going to "get it" any time
soon, because in fact "no" *didn't* mean no. There always seemed
to be more for the company to give. If you're discouraged by
hearing "no" for an answer, then maybe negotiations are not the
place for you. Remember the lesson from "everything is negotiable" (i.e., of pushing the envelope, testing the parameters).
The same applies to "no."

When you are at the beginning of a negotiation—especially
a complex negotiation—there can be literally hundreds of is-

sues. When you first meet with your counterparts and they review their positions, they will no doubt note that they are without movement on a host of those issues. Do not waste your time or energy arguing with them or trying to persuade them at the outset. Just note their comments and use the time for them to review the issues and their concerns. Negotiations can be a time-consuming process and you need to begin the process of peeling away the layers of the onion, to test the depth of your counterparts' commitment on each issue (see chapter 4). Hopefully you will spend time on that process and build the relationship as you go. Along the way, you will find solutions to some of these problems that they've identified as intractable. Make it clear at the outset that your silence should not imply assent. Let them know that when you nod your head up and down, it is to say that you hear them and understand their concerns. It does not mean that you agree. Then proceed to patiently listen. Do not—do not—engage your counterparts at the outset on these issues. They will fall soon enough. In fact, if one truism emerges from negotiations, it is that the issue that is identified by your counterparts as the issue with the least movement will almost surely fall, although usually at the end.

Which brings us to our next rule.

The Pressure on the Last Issue Is Great: In the context of a hundred issues, saying "no" to issue #38—or #54, or #92—is meaningless. As the number of issues diminishes, "no" becomes marginally more important. Saying, "hell, no" to one of two remaining issues is quite serious, but still not determinative, as you'll see in a later example. As you move through the negotiation, settling dozens of issues that seemed insurmountable at one time or another, you begin to build the relationship and build confidence, but difficult issues always remain. The pres-

111

sure to resolve these last issues—and indeed to resolve the last issue—is great.

The last issue becomes known as the "deal-breaker." That's it. It's the one with the power to bring down the whole deal. It is contentious, of that you can be certain. Yet, its power cuts both ways. For while the parties may not want to compromise on it, they must be willing to sacrifice all for it, too. A union negotiator can stand firm on an issue, but that is different from asking his or her members to forego a paycheck, to go on strike over it. So, too, a management negotiator can assure his CEO that he or she will not relent on a given issue, but will the CEO be willing to shut down the company over that issue? If it's the last remaining issue, they'd better be ready to sacrifice all, or else it must be compromised. However, there is a caution here: Be careful which issue you leave until last. If it's an issue on which you *really* don't want to compromise, but over which your organization is not willing to fight to the death, then you'd better figure out a way to settle it. If it begins to look as though it will hang out there by itself, the pressure on you to settle it will be enormous. It will not only be the "deal breaker," it will potentially be the "deal maker" as well.

In other words, if you leave an issue until last, do it with your eyes wide open, with the full knowledge of the pressure that will be brought to bear on the issue. Don't leave a troublesome issue until last just because you prefer not to deal with it. The pressure on that issue can turn it against you just as easily as it can turn it in your favor.

I had a case involving the smallest union of three at a medium-sized company. They were new on the property and had only recently won their election. This was their first contract. They had negotiated dutifully with the company through dozens and dozens of issues. Toward the end of the negotiations, there

*remained only a few issues: pay, pensions, health care, and union
security. The first three are obvious. The last one dealt with
whether everyone at the company would be required to join the
union as a condition of employment and pay dues to the union.
The company was still angry that the union won the election, so
they just didn't want to agree to the last issue at all.*

*The parties began to creep closer toward agreement on the
other—quite major—issues. Soon, it looked as though they had
an agreement in principle on all three: pay, pensions, and health
care. To my surprise, the union refused to sign off on them and
kept them "open" for further discussion. Finally, I understood
their reluctance. Since they were new to the company, their political support among the members was a little thin. If the union
ever had to use the ultimate weapon, the strike, they needed to
make sure they wielded that weapon with the full support of
their membership. It would be easy to persuade their members
to strike over wages, pensions, and health care. It was unlikely
that they would be able to drum up any support for a strike over
union security, about which this group cared little.*

*As a result, the union carefully kept negotiating over the key
issues—kept them open, in other words—in the interest of trying to package the union security issue with one of the economic issues. Only after they were able to do this would they
agree to a final deal with the company.*

This next scenario illustrates the twin points of leaving an
issue until last and the perils of taking a counterpart's word that
"no" meant no.

*One issue in this negotiation—we'll call it Issue X—had
emerged from the company side as a clear and unequivocal "hell,
no." Time and time again, the company negotiator had told the
union negotiator that they had absolutely no intention of making any concessions on Issue X. At the end of the negotiation,*

only a handful of issues remained. In the small group was an issue of vital importance to the union, which the company had similarly rejected, and Issue X. The union negotiator, who was seasoned and smart, took his issue and packaged it with Issue X. He knew that this meant that finally, at last, he would gain the issue he really wanted. Surely, he told the company, you must give in on one of these issues, since you've been intransigent on both and there are only a few issues remaining.

To his complete surprise, the company relented and gave in on Issue X. It was, as it turns out, less important to them than the issue the union wanted. In fact, at that point, the union really didn't care whether the company gave in on Issue X. They really wanted the other item. No matter, the uninon negotiator was hoisted by his own petard for wrapping the two issues together. To his shock—and mine—they relented on Issue X. "No" really didn't mean no after all. He left these two issues until last and packaged them in such a way as to force the company to accept his issue. Yet, he took the company at their word and believed that their "hell, no" was immutable. It wasn't.

I learned that day that you just can't count on people to stay wedded to their positions.

Be Persistent: As is probably clear from the previous discussion (i.e., that "final" doesn't mean final and "no" doesn't mean no), persistence figures quite prominently in negotiations. Those who are easily turned away by a "no" or who too easily accept the price that is quoted or the parameters that are given have no place in this game of persistence and endurance.

So much of negotiation, as noted above, is endurance, just sitting in the chair and grinding it out, building the relationship as you go. High-profile negotiations attract media and public attention at the eleventh and twelfth hours. It is both tense and exciting at those moments. But what the public doesn't see is that these people have been negotiating often for months or even years. They have spent long, tedious hours going through arcane and technical issues, making small compromises and slowly inching toward agreement.

The flip side of endurance, of course, is patience. One must be possessed of enormous patience to sit through, to endure, lengthy negotiations, which often move at a snail's pace. Don't be impatient. You will reach your goal soon enough. Don't attempt to force it or to make shortcuts. Although it is tedious, you are building trust, building the relationship.

Persistence, too, is a great quality in any negotiator. When told "no"—or even "hell, no"—you must continue to make another pass at the issue, to try, try again. Don't ever give up until the final deal is signed. When all seems lost, when the night is darkest, that is when your persistence will pay off. It is too easy as a negotiator or a mediator to grow discouraged when a party tells you they won't meet or they won't yield on an issue. You must give them alternatives, give them context, show them you are focused in your desire to attain that item, whatever it may be. Be respectful of their view, but be persistent, even relentless.

I was involved in the mother of all disputes at Eastern Air Lines (EAL) back in the late 1980s. It had a long and torrid history, with great and seemingly insoluble enmity between labor and management. The unions had made safety a priority issue with their members, the press, and the traveling public. Then-Secretary of Transportation Jim Burnley asked former Secretary of Labor (and my friend and mentor) Bill Brock to act as a special mediator on safety issues, to ensure that the labor–management bitterness did not spill over into safety. Brock drafted me from my safe enclave at the Labor Department, and

I was detailed for the summer of 1988 to the Department of Transportation to assist Brock in this quixotic task.

We toiled virtually around the clock for months, traveling around the EAL system, meeting with groups of employees, both labor and management, hearing their complaints and gaining their insights. As is the case with even the greatest and most bitter disputes, we heard virtually the same complaints from everyone, and they were all fairly mundane and eminently "fixable." Go to the world's worst labor dispute and you'll probably find a water fountain that needs to be fixed, that's been neglected by management. It is amazing but often true. Mediators expect insurmountable issues, but it's the minutia, the every day nuisance or oversight, that irks the workers. EAL was no different.

Brock and I drafted a series of accords that addressed the parties' complaints. The accords were drafted with the input of the parties and were thoroughly vetted with them ad nauseam over a period of weeks to make sure the language was right and that it was something to which they could all agree. Having expended Herculean efforts to gain their assent in advance, we figured it was time for a meeting of all the principals. The object was to gain their official agreement—and signatures—on all these documents and then to announce and go forward with these "safety accords," labor and management together. Given their history, the fact that they would do anything jointly we hoped would speak volumes and start them on their way to a fuller peace.

To my knowledge, this was the only meeting ever attended by Frank Lorenzo and all three union chiefs. Two of Lorenzo's top executives accompanied him to the meeting. We met in the Transportation Secretary's elegant, oak-paneled conference room, with all its attendant pomp and circumstance. Around the table sat all the protagonists of this Hundred Years' War, with all the baggage and history they could bring.

Brock opened the meeting and reviewed the work we had done thus far. He passed out sets of the documents—about ten pages in all—to each of the participants. None of them was seeing these documents for the first time. All had reviewed and cleared them in advance. If all went according to plan, this meeting should last less than a half hour.

Brock waited to make sure all the parties had the paper in front of them. "OK," he said, "Let's review these documents." He looked around the room. "Any comments on page one?" he asked. He looked to his right, to go around the table in order.

"No comment" said the company, "Looks fine to us." Brock looked next at union number 1.

"We'd like to change a word in the last paragraph," they said, and it was not a big deal to anyone. He looked at union number 2, who simply nodded their assent. He looked finally at union number 3.

"This is a whitewash!" their leader hollered as he pounded the table. "We're being railroaded into signing something we don't want to sign!" He was only warming up. "This process stinks!" he shouted, "And we refuse to be a part of it!"

You can imagine how I felt. I had put every minute of my life into this for months. The involved parties had called me at home at midnight, at 6 A.M., and at all times in between. This was too important to leave to chance, so we carefully made sure everyone would be on board before we ever called this meeting. But now, it was clear that union number 3 was having buyer's remorse and was not willing to be part of any deal. Since that was the case, this process was over. It would not work unless all three unions were part of the deal. Two out of three gained us nothing, no peace. It was over. I remember sitting there, stunned, *with my world crashing in around me. Everything I had worked so hard to achieve had been dashed in that one moment by the sole unwilling participant. I recall laying down my pen and reaching slowly for my bag, knowing it was time to go.*

The next words I heard were Brock's.

"Page two?" he said, and looked back to his right at the company. I was astounded. Brock had been a member of Congress, a U.S. Senator, Chairman of the GOP, U.S. Trade Representative, and Secretary of Labor. He had a stellar résumé, but at this moment, I could not believe he could be so stupid. Had he not heard union number 3? Did he not understand the implications of the comment? Without union number 3, we were dead in the water and they knew it. This was a calculated move and they weren't about to change their view. Going past this point was a clear waste of time. Still, given his stature and the uncertainty swirling about the room at that time, the company had no choice but to answer. They offered up a small word change. Union number 1 passed and union number 2 had another small change, to which the others agreed. When he came to union number 3, their leader spoke anew.

"This process stinks!" he said again. "It's a whitewash! I'm being railroaded into a process I want nothing to do with!" He finished again by saying he refused to be a part of the process. However "over" I considered the meeting to be after his first objection, it was clearly over at this point. This time, I had a chance to watch the dynamics. Brock, a wonderfully understated and sincere man, just stared at union number 3 and nodded. He was not dismissive, he was respectful. He heard their concerns, but didn't answer them or meet them in any way. I laughed to myself, at the absurdity of it all when I heard Brock say, "Page three?" and look at the company.

They had no changes, union number 1 had a small change,

and union number 2 had no changes. Brock looked at union number 3.

"I think the second to the last word in the second paragraph should be changed to 'may'" he said.

He was in.

At that moment, union number 3 bought into the process. I had all I could do to keep from cheering aloud. It was such an incredible relief. However, Brock betrayed no emotion, said nothing to note their change of heart. He just calmly noted their change and looked again to his right at the company and said, "Page four?" We spent another hour or more discussing the rest of the document, but it was all pretty amicable from there. Had I been in charge, I would have engaged union number 3 on their first objection, would have argued with them publicly, would have cemented their opposition, and would have destroyed the entire process. What Brock did was listen respectfully without giving undue weight to their concerns. After all, there were three other parties in the room, and they had all worked earnestly on these documents, they had all made concessions, and they all had a view, a shared hope for some measure of peace. This was their process, too.

But most important, that day I learned the value of persistence. An unseasoned negotiator would have just walked away—as I would have on that day—thinking that in fact it was over. It wasn't over. Brock simply persisted and persisted and negotiated his way through it all.

We didn't save Eastern Air Lines, but on that day, at that moment, the sun shone oh so briefly.

Time and time again in a negotiation, it can appear as if all is lost, as if you and your counterpart are out of moves. You must remember John Belushi in the film, *Animal House*, screaming, "It's never over!" You can't give up, walk away. You must meet with your counterpart, rehash old issues, old arguments. Too many times, parties come away from those meetings with new insights. Ask again what their objections are to your proposal, and tell them your objections to theirs again. Very frequently in the retelling of the issues, the interests, parties stumble upon some crack in the wall through which shines the light of hope.

The closest I ever came to a strike—without having one— was on a case involving a small company and its largest union. It had been a long and contentious negotiation and we had ne- gotiated for three days—seventy-two continuous hours—past the strike deadline in the hopes of getting a deal, but hopes were growing increasingly dim. The company negotiator and the chief union negotiator were old friends. Out of tricks, I spoke to them separately before I put them together—alone—in a side room away from their respective groups. I told the lead com- pany negotiator to "open his wallet" and to let his old friend know how far he could go in this agreement—the time for pos- turing, for game-playing, had long since passed. For his part, I told the union chief he needed to be frank with his friend and counterpart and let him know what he really needed out of this deal. Since I knew they had to save face even with me, I did not join them.

They sat in there alone for about half an hour. When they emerged, both their faces were somber. The company negotia- tor caught my eye and just shook his head sadly from side to side. It was clear to me that the end was near. The union nego- tiator spoke first and told me they had a friendly and honest discussion, but they were still very far apart and there was no way that they could bridge the gap. They stood in the hallway for a moment, pondering the inevitable. They decided they needed to summon their lawyers (who had accompanied them to the negotiations) to have a brief but official conversation with one another, so that the end of negotiations could be called and the strike could begin.

The company's caucus room was nearby and I watched as the company negotiator walked into the room and gave them the bad news. His lawyer dutifully walked toward my office. However, as an afterthought, he stopped in the doorway to his room and summoned Pete to come with him "as a witness." Pete was a young guy who had only recently moved from the ranks of this particular union into management. He was being groomed for more responsible management positions, and so they brought him along to be an observer at these negotiations, so he could begin his learning process. He had no official function. He was a supernumerary, a cast member with no speaking role. The lawyer wanted him in the room only to check his version of events, should they later find themselves in litigation. Together, they walked into my office. We milled about for a few minutes waiting for the union to arrive. I stood next to Pete in the hallway while we waited.

"I've seen the strike plan," he said to me, ashen. "It's terrible." He told me the company planned in the case of a strike to have a virtual shutdown and instantly to lay off most of the employees. This company had been in a fairly fragile financial state, and thus a short shutdown meant that many people would not be rehired if and when the strike ended and the company reopened for business. He told me he had urged the company to share the strike plan with the union, so they could see for themselves how horrible it would be, but the company decided against it. It was their considered judgment that rather than moving the union toward an agreement, it would be seen as a threat and would enrage them, driving them further apart. It was a plausible interpretation, a reasonable fear. Still, Pete had seen the strike plan and was clearly unnerved.

In only a few moments the union lawyer and the chief union negotiator walked into the room. The mood was deeply somber and we were all exhausted. I reviewed the bidding and told them where we were. They were all impatient. The two union reps had told their committee that they would only be a moment and the strike would begin. Their committee waited nervously for their prompt return. For my part, there was no way I was going to let any of these people out of my office.

I asked them, à la Detective Colombo, to outline for me again the issues that separated them, even though I knew them by heart. They were exasperated with me, and their answers were curt and heated. Still, I pressed them. There were no rabbits left in my hat, the only thin reed of hope to which I clung was that somewhere in this discussion they might find some area of agreement that had somehow eluded them for the previous seventy-two hours. But it was not to be. We rehashed all the issues to the edge of their nerves and back. The union lawyer looked at the company lawyer and nodded knowingly, as if to say, "Let's get on with it." The company lawyer nodded back. It was over at last.

At that moment a new voice interrupted. "Can I say something?"

We all stopped what we were doing and looked at Pete. He was looking at me, seeking my permission. I knew he was not supposed to speak, that his lawyer didn't want him to speak, only to witness the course of events, but at that point, the time for diplomacy had passed. "Sure," I said and looked around the room for an objection. Finding none, he proceeded to speak.

His voice was low and measured. "Look," he said, "I'm the only company employee in this room." He noted his own lawyer, an outside counsel, and the two union representatives, one outside lawyer and the other who worked for the union. As for me, I worked for the U.S. Government.

"I'm the only person here who works for this company," he continued, "and let me tell you what a strike will mean to my company," he gulped hard, "and to my friends." He began to talk softly but with intense passion about how hard he and his colleagues had worked to build the company, how it was their company, and how they had taken great pride in it. He said that a strike would ruin the company for all time and with it, many lives. As he spoke, tears streamed down his cheeks. It was the most powerful thing I had ever witnessed in negotiations. In a world full of posturing, this was real emotion.

He spoke for only a few minutes, I suppose. When he finished, the room was dead silent. Pete wiped his eyes and stared at the floor. No one wanted to be the first to speak.

After several moments the union lawyer spoke. She addressed the theological issue that had separated them from the start. She spoke softly, as if in church, and offered an idea that had not yet been discussed, a way of solving the issue by putting it off until the next negotiations and agreeing to study the options jointly in the interim. She asked plaintively what the company might do on wages if the union would agree to defer the theological issue in this way. The company negotiator, who was a real pro, jumped in and began to outline a framework for a solution on wages. They all began sketching boxes in the air, putting this issue here, and these two over here, and this one down here. They talked for another half hour or so and then agreed to take a break. As we sat back, we realized that both committees had been sitting in their respective caucus rooms, waiting for them to return from a five-minute pro forma meeting and this was nearly ninety minutes later. I discovered later that in fact both sides had called back to their respective bases to let them know the strike was beginning.

We pulled everyone back together—by now it was 3 A.M.—

and I got out of the way as paper flew mightily back and be-tween them, and they settled issues left and right. By 7 A.M., they were done, they had their deal.

In the haze of the deal, the union negotiator, an old hand himself, came up to me and told me this was the closest he had ever come to a strike without actually having one. He had been involved in dozens and dozens of negotiations, but had never seen one this close to going over the edge.

In both the previous examples, the value of persistence in negotiations is clear. In both examples, inexperienced negotiators would have walked away, thinking a deal elusive or impossible. Yet if you want to reach an agreement, you must be tenacious, a terrier with a bone. You must not let it go. If it appears that you are at the end, ask your counterparts to review again with you the reasons why it is over. As in the last example, they may grow exasperated and tell you they've been over it a million times but you must persist. Again, it is not uncommon in meetings of that type for parties to stumble upon an opening, a crack in the door wide enough through which to talk. In reviewing the bidding and their positions, parties often uncover a fundamental misunderstanding or a ray of hope that had eluded them until then. You must stay glued to your chair and persevere. To quote the great Yogi Berra, "It ain't over 'til it's over." It's your job to make sure it is never over until the deal is done.

"Noise" Is Part of the Process: "Noise" in this context is intended broadly to mean a whole host of wailing and gnashing of teeth. In a nonlabor setting, it might take the form of rhetoric or posturing, or walking away from a negotiation, or conde-scension, or petulance. In labor settings, noise usually trans-lates into decibels. It can become quite heated, and tempers and voices can rise. The introductory chapter mentioned the parallel to nuclear physics. Bodies must discharge energy before they can move, and they do. This translates into noise, plain and simple.

As a negotiator, there is only one thing you can do with noise: Ignore it. That's right, you must walk away from it. If you engage it, you will lose your focus, lose your balance. You must not let yourself grow distracted, you must keep your eye on the prize, on getting a deal. If your counterpart resorts to any form of noise, ignore it. Imagine you are an actor playing a role, if you must. The other side is screaming at the person in your position, not at you. Let it go.

As a mediator as well, you should also be aware of another great truism of negotiations: Parties will yell at one another for only a finite—and generally brief—period of time. The first time you are in a room where someone is raising his voice, you imagine his ability to continue is limitless, and the prospects of that are truly dreadful. Mediators typically jump in at that point. However, over time, one realizes that indeed there is a definite limit to how long people can yell, typically only a few minutes. Those minutes will seem like an eternity, but they really are only a few minutes. After that time the parties usually cease, out of relief and embarrassment. But often, the skies clear after such an episode and the parties can move ahead.

I received a call from a management consultant for a small, family-owned business. She said she was in need of a mediator to serve as a facilitator or intermediary in a dispute involving the CEO (who was a member of the family that owned the company) and the chief financial officer, who had been hired from outside. The consultant warned me in her voice-mail message that they needed a mediator because things otherwise "might get heated."

When I called her back, she gave me many details. This conflict had raged for years and years, apparently. To their credit, both sides had agreed to the use of a mediator to help them discuss their differences. I told the management consultant that without knowing the parties, my gut instinct was to let them speak their minds and to let them argue a bit—through many generations and iterations, no doubt—to clear the air. I told the consultant of my rule (i.e., that they won't scream at each other forever). It'll only last a while. But I also warned her that if it started, time wouldn't exactly fly. It would seem like an eternity that they were arguing, but it sounded to me as though that sort of eruption was about twenty years overdue.

Noise is an integral part of the negotiating process, because it is the result of a release of energy, of frustration, from people who are coming to grips with the fact that they can't gain everything they want from this negotiation. It's common, don't let it distract you.

One important caveat, however, and that is the difference between the noise of frustration and the noise of intimidation. Parties often blow off steam in frustration. Often, it's not directed at their counterpart and it is typically unintentional. However, the noise of intimidation is directed at one's counterpart —and often at mediators—to catch them off guard and is intentional. Again, in either case, you must employ the same defense, that is, ignore it. Don't borrow trouble in the case of your frustrated counterpart and in the case of your intimidator, don't give him or her the victory.

Negotiations Are 50 Percent Psychology and 50 Percent Sales:
That half of negotiations which are psychology should be evident from everything you have read thus far. Issues like empathy, finding common ground, saving face, and so forth, are all elements of

the psychological game that underlies every negotiation. A negotiator who ignores issues like ego and power is sure to suffer some tough sledding as a result.

While many professional negotiators (and mediators) are lawyers by training, psychology may be the better discipline to prepare one for a life as a negotiator. Some of the best books on negotiation urge negotiators to put personalities aside. However, in most circumstances, this is almost impossible to do. It is better to learn the personalities and their particular "hot buttons" and motivations, their styles and what best persuades them (e.g., the empirical or the empathetic) and act accordingly. Assuming for the moment that you are human, you will find it difficult to put personalities aside, especially the difficult ones.

You need to know what your counterparts' "drivers" are, that is, what motivates them, what their concerns are. Once you learn this, you must use some psychology to bring them around to your way of thinking. You must be always mindful of the balance of power and aware that people don't want to feel powerless, whether they are in fact powerless or not. This, then, is the psychology of negotiations: the understanding of the sub rosa, the undercurrents, the external pressures present in every negotiation, and acting accordingly.

The other side of the coin is sales.

It is astounding how little true dialogue happens in any negotiation. Parties play defense, but they don't play offense very often. That is, they argue with their counterpart and point out the flaws in their proposal, but neither side spends an inordinate amount of time selling the positive points of their own proposal. In a labor negotiation, parties push back and forth huge proposals, big stacks of paper. While they might spend some time on the "what," that is, on the elements of the proposal, they typically don't spend very much time on the "why," that is, why did you make this proposal? What is it based on? While the size of the proposal may differ, this element is true in most negotiations. People exchange their ideas, their view of beauty, and let the other side read it and draw their own conclusions on motive. If you are to be an effective negotiator, you must not only be a defender, but you must be an advocate as well. Advocate your point of view and engage your counterparts in dialogue about what they like and don't like about your proposal. There are far too many gaps in communications to simply leave it to chance.

If your proposal is based on nothing, was just picked out of thin air, shame on you. In most cases, your proposal is based on some degree of thought and research and homework. Let your counterpart know what thoughts, what information went into your proposal and how you drew your conclusions. In a labor negotiation, if you're offering a 3 percent wage increase, don't just put it in your 150-page proposal with the other issues and let your counterparts think what they will. Let them know, for example, that this is the industry average, that it will still put them at the top of the industry in pay, that it will result in their members being the highest-paid in that region or that state. If you're offering 10 percent less than the asking price for a house, let the sellers know, for example, that the comparable prices in the neighborhood don't support a higher bid. The house is older, and—you've calculated—will need about $20,000 worth of repairs and replacements in the next year. Merely to send in a bid that's 10 percent lower than the asking price, without an explanation, can often have the effect of offending the sellers. You need to create the context and let them know what it is—actually say it. It is rare that people will actually do this. Typically, people negotiate by simply tossing out dueling numbers at one another. You need to have a discussion and to use it to sell and to learn the reasons behind your counterpart's point of view as well. It's O.K. to want something just because you want it, but it's much harder actually to get it, unless you can persuade your counterpart to compromise or relent.

As a mediator, I would sit through long sessions with the parties and listen to them argue with one another at length about their proposals, each side attacking the other. The discussions were often conducted in short bursts, with each side simply defending their position. When the parties would break, it was typical for both sides to talk to me much more openly. "I can't believe they didn't accept our proposal," they'd say, agitated, "This will give them the richest pension in the industry, far ahead of our competitors!"

I'd always look at them and say the same thing: "Don't tell me—tell them!" Parties seemed to save their most persuasive arguments for me, the mediator, out of earshot of their counterpart. At core, I guess some believed their counterpart wasn't interested in hearing their rationale. You need to make sure they're interested and spell it out for them.

Don't just make proposals, *sell* them to your counterpart. It may look as if they don't care, or as if they're not listening, but they do and they are. In labor negotiations, labor will use all of management's arguments when they take the tentative agreement out to be ratified by their full membership. Time and again, the very arguments that the company used in negotiations—and that the union seemed to dismiss at the time—were also used in the documents that the union sent out to "sell" the contract to its members. Remember that there are layers of interests, and remember that everyone has a boss. The better you sell your proposal, the more ammunition you've given your counterparts to sell it to their boss.

Don't Negotiate, Mediate: People who negotiate become completely wrapped up in the roles they inhabit. That is, if they are union negotiators, they become completely caught up in that role. So, too, with company negotiators or anyone who is wed to a particular position on any given day. Yet in so many cases, a person's point of view is wed more to the accident of birth than to any particular ideology. That is, fate put you where you happen to be negotiating that day. Imagine that one day when you show up to negotiate, fate has stepped in and instead made you the mediator. What would you do (other than complain loudly, of course)? You would have to brainstorm. You would have to listen to what each party was saying and try to find solutions, middle ground. You would have to absorb conflict, not exacerbate it. You would look for any semblance of common ground between the two parties (see chapter 6, Mediators: Lessons and Observations). Why not do this as the negotiator?

It is a tactic employed by very few negotiators, but those who use it have great success. They talk in terms of "our" problem (i.e., theirs and their counterparts'). They say they understand their counterparts' problem and they brainstorm with them to find a solution. They work together at every turn, allied against The Problem—whatever it may be—to attack it and to solve it. In short, they set themselves up as the mediator. This is enormously effective.

Only once in my life have I had the great misfortune of being named as a defendant in a lawsuit. For those of you who have been through it, you know how dreadful it can be. As a mediator, I found it doubly bad for me in that once the process began, I and my codefendants lost all control over the case, and it was in the hands of the lawyers, who seemed to enjoy spending our money to spar over arcane legal theories. Perhaps another book will follow on that topic, but for this book the relevant part of the suit is that a year into the litigation, my partners and I found ourselves in a two-hour mediation session mandated by the court.

On one side of the table were two of my partners and I and our lawyer. On the other side was our landlord and his lawyer. At the end of the table was the mediator, a kind but inexperienced attorney, who was a volunteer. The landlord and I were seated directly across from one another. It was clear from the outset that the lawyers—ours and theirs—were there only because they were required by the court to be there. They had no interest in settling, and I could slowly feel our money and our lives draining away. The first ninety minutes of the meeting sped by with the lawyers arguing and presenting their view of the facts.

Knowing there was only a short time left and fearing we would end without really trying to settle the case, I injected myself into the process. As I began to speak, our lawyer turned ashen. The first thing I did was look across the table at our landlord, a decent, honest man with whom we had enjoyed a good relationship until a great misunderstanding a year before. I looked him in the eye and apologized to him for all the trouble we had caused him. I offered a brief explanation of the reasons behind our actions—reasons he had not heard before that moment—and told him we were all very sorry that we had put him in this position. It was at about this point that our lawyer tried to silence me once again, but I was relentless.

I told the landlord that he and we were in the same position that day in that the longer he stayed in that room, the more it was going to cost him, since his lawyer was charging him a hefty fee. The same applied to us, I reminded him, and we were also losing money by being kept away from our jobs—and our clients—for the duration. The mediator was a volunteer, I reminded him, so she wasn't making any money either. The only two people in the room making money, I said, were the lawyers, and they were the only two who appeared to have no interest in settling. Finally, I reminded him that we were just a small corporation with no great assets and that any settlement would be paid personally by those of us around the table. It wasn't theory or insurance. It was our money, it was personal.

I took out a scrap of paper and scribbled some numbers, based on comments he had made, outlining his out-of-pocket losses as a result of our actions. I looked him in the eye and passed it across the table to him. He took it and perused it and nodded. His lawyer grabbed it out of his hand, looked it over and threw it back across the table at me. "We're not interested!" he shouted at me. I calmly took the piece of paper, never took my eyes off of the landlord, and passed it back to him and he calmly retrieved it and reviewed it again.

His lawyer kept hectoring me, so I shouted an invective at him, which frightened everyone in the room but succeeded in keeping him completely at bay for the remainder of the session. I learned that one from watching many union negotiators. With his lawyer at bay, the landlord had a chance to review and mull over the proposal and eventually nodded across the table at me. We had our deal.

The above scenario is a personal example of negotiator as mediator. In this particular case, there was even a mediator in the room, but left to his own devices, a mediator might not push the envelope, either. Had all in the room chosen to stick to their assigned roles, the day would have ended without a deal. It was for the lawyers to negotiate, for the parties to observe, and for the mediator to mediate. In the best case, the parties might have been able to negotiate, but only for the purposes of advancing and reinforcing their position and for preserving their litigation posture. The negotiator as mediator here achieved a few objectives: it helped establish common ground between the parties (the economic interests of the parties vs. the lawyers), the tone was set (i.e., through the apology), and there was some brainstorming to find a solution. You can—and should—do the same thing when negotiating. Establish yourself as the mediator, establish common ground, set the tone, and brainstorm to find solutions to the problems that you and your counterpart share.

Here's another example, this one of a group that was seeking a mediator and found one in the most unlikely place.

I was contacted by a large association (A) that was caught in crossfire between two other groups (B and C). B and C were warring, and their conflict was having a great and negative economic impact on Group A. For their part, Group A did not have entirely clean hands in this process and were themselves a bit at war with both B and C. Group A was eager to bring me into the dispute to mediate, but I had several concerns, not the least of which was that they were parties to the dispute and were aiming to force their choice of a mediator (i.e., me) on the other two groups. Even with full disclosure, I was concerned. As a result, I demurred, but agreed to help Group A navigate through the dispute. They never quite took "no" for an answer and continued to lobby me to mediate whenever we met, but I continued to demur.

At each meeting, a top executive from Group A would tell me all the dynamics of the two groups, the issues, the politics, their economic and personal interests, and so on. We met several times over several weeks, and each time he would walk me through another aspect, another angle of the dispute. One night over dinner, he gave me what he believed to be the outlines of a possible deal. To my surprise, he mentioned that at the very beginning of the dispute, both Group B and Group C had come to see him separately and had given him some idea of what each could accept in a deal with the other. Furthermore, throughout this entire dispute, he had stayed in relatively constant contact with the heads of Groups B and C and was on fairly amicable terms with them both.

"I think we found a mediator," I told him, but at first it didn't sink in, and he stared at me blankly.

"You!" I said, to his utter shock and maybe revulsion. It was true, he was a bit of a party to this dispute, but he was also in the best position to mediate it in that he had the relationship with the heads of the other groups and had a good idea of what both could and couldn't accept. I urged him to get on a plane and go play "what if" with the heads of both groups.

In a traditional sense, the gentleman in the above scenario would never be a mediator. He was a partisan and was a quasi-party to this very dispute. Yet once we broke out of that mindset of thinking of people in clear lines with clearly defined expectations and roles, we were free to think a little creatively about dispute resolution and problem solving. Furthermore, appointing him mediator had the additional benefit of taking Groups B and C by surprise because they never expected him to be constructive. When he was, they were very willing to talk to him and to let him lead them toward agreement.

Next time you find yourself negotiating, try mediating instead.

Momentum Is in Favor of an Agreement: It is important to note when you begin a negotiation that in all likelihood, you will come to agreement with your counterpart. The roots of this likelihood are in our culture. We are a peace-loving, conflict-averse country. Not all cultures share this trait, and in some other countries, dispute resolution is a different game altogether. Here in this country, hope can be low at the beginning of a negotiation, and it is often difficult to see where the process might lead. However, in almost all cases, you are at the table (whether or not there's an actual table) because you and your counterpart want to try to reach an agreement. Once you begin with that premise, agreement typically follows—not always easily, mind you, and not always immediately, but it follows. Deals break down in only a very small minority of cases. When you're at your darkest hour, just remind yourself that the odds of your gaining an agreement are quite favorable.

You Don't Have to Make a Bad Deal: All the preceding notwithstanding, you don't ever need to make a bad deal. Yes, you should be single-minded about concluding a deal, keeping your eye on the prize, remembering that your goal is to drain the swamp. Yes, momentum greatly favors ultimately getting there. However, it is not your job to do it at all costs. At the end of the day, you must step back and assess the deal you're about to sign in terms of your original list of "gottas" and "wannas." You need to see whether you gained as much from the agreement as you could have and whether you kept your concessions to a minimum. If you are truly at the end, and you've exhausted all possible avenues, and the negotiating is truly over, you must evaluate the value of the deal to you, its net gains and losses. If it simply does not add up, that is, if it is simply not in your best interests to sign it, don't sign it. Again, this will happen only in a very small minority of cases, but when it does, you must learn to walk away. You should be making a deal but you should be making a good deal. You need not make a bad deal, just to make a deal.

Probably the most predominant way that people make a bad deal is when they become emotionally wed to the goal. "The mind" goes the adage, "is always fool to the heart." Nowhere is this truer than in negotiations. Whether the item is an *objet d'art*, a house, or a snazzy red sports car, once you become emotionally wed to it, all is lost. In other words, you must be able to walk away from whatever it is that is the subject of the negotiation. Put in the terms of this book, if the only "gotta" on your list is the object itself, the car, the house, and there are no "wannas" with which to negotiate, your leverage begins to slip away. It evaporates completely at the point your counterpart realizes you are wed to the object of the negotiation.

Experience shows there are very few "one of a kind" items. The cute Tudor with the white picket fence may pale in comparison to another house that may become available if you wait just a bit longer. The snazzy red sports car actually is improved in the next model year, you discover. You'll almost always have another bite at this or a similar apple. Keep you emotions in check, keep your wits about you, and don't let your heart steer you into a bad deal.

Chapter 6

Mediators: Lessons and Observations

This chapter is for mediators real and aspiring and for negotiators who seek to employ some "mediator as negotiator" tactics. It is a review of the role of the mediator and includes some rules for mediators, too.

The mediator has many roles: whipping boy, midwife, font of all wisdom and creative solutions, sorcerer's apprentice, and lightning rod. Parties grow so weary of arguing with one another that they turn instantly to the mediator once he becomes involved. A mediator does not always descend into the fray like an archangel bathed in white light. Often he is in the mud with the parties, taking his share of heat and attack.

Above all, however, the mediator is a neutral and must project neutrality in all he does. He must let the slings and arrows of the parties glance off of him. They are intended to keep him off balance and must be ignored. As noted above, the energy in any dispute must go somewhere. A healthy share of it ultimately finds its way to the mediator, who must ignore it.

Near the deadline of a dispute the parties are under enormous pressure from their constituency, whoever that might be. There is much at stake. In the midst of that pressure cooker sits the mediator pushing and prodding both sides toward agreement. They are already under enough stress, they don't need any more. The mediator picks up his share of the heat from the parties as a result. Karl Wallenda, father of the circus high-wire family that bears his name, says, "Walking the high wire is living. All else is waiting." For the true mediator, this eleventh or twelfth hour—as emotionally charged and explosive as it is—is living. All else is waiting.

A mediator can be either the most powerful or most power-less person in the room, depending on the circumstances. A mediator ultimately has as much authority as the parties will give him. No independent enforcement authority is invested in a mediator. Sometimes a mediator will order the parties to do something and they'll comply, and sometimes they'll totally ignore him. There is no grail there. The parties decide how much deference to give the mediator. Mediators are everlastingly us-ing their wit and guile, cajoling the parties, and using their pow-ers of persuasion to move people toward doing something they'd rather not do. Sometimes parties are willing participants, and sometimes they negotiate kicking and screaming.

For any mediator—or any neutral—there are some essential rules. They must always be attempted, but are probably never fully achieved.

Project Neutrality in All You Do: Neutrality is easily said, not so easily achieved. Assuming you are human and that your parties are also human, it is the hardest thing to do. It is impossible to like everyone. In fact, you don't have to like them, only endure them for a finite period of time. Still, you will run across personality types that you find reprehensible.

One of my first cases as an arbitrator involved a consumer dispute. On one side of the table sat the sweetest elderly couple you could imagine. They owned a very inexpensive car, and it was their only car. As it turns out, they were not retired, but were still working in spite of the fact that both were near seventy. He worked days and she worked nights as a waitress. It was the dead of winter and she was getting into the car to go to work, late at night. He was dutifully helping her into the car. Her coat caught the turn signal on the steering wheel and broke it off. The cost of the repair was more than they could afford, and they had come to arbitration to see whether the automaker would pay for the repair, because of an inherent manufacturer's defect.

Across the table from them sat one of the vilest men I have ever encountered. He sat (in the dead of winter) with a shirt open almost to his navel, and wore his sunglasses throughout the hearing. He drummed his fingers nervously on the table the entire time he sat there. Every few minutes—especially during their presentation of the facts—he'd interrupt to say, "I think we've heard enough. I think we can get out of here." I kept urging him to be quiet and not to interrupt. In response, he would exhale loudly, signaling his exasperation. I would then invite the elderly couple (who held hands during most of the hearing) to continue.

There couldn't have been a more stark contrast between characters sympathetic and unsympathetic. Still, as the case pro-

gressed, it seemed clear to me that this really wasn't the manufacturer's fault. I knew I was probably not going to award the couple anything. The part was not defective, and my job was not to do income redistribution based on personalities and sympathies, as much as I might have wanted to do so.

However, in a tip of my hat to some semblance of humanity, I let them go on at length, just to unnerve the company representative. I couldn't help it—he was such a rude and base individual. The only leverage I had was to make him sit and stew, and I did. It might have been a sign of my own immaturity at the time, but I'd probably do the same thing today.

You will meet some very unpleasant personality types as you mediate. You must tolerate them and treat them as you do everyone else, hard as it is.

I once had a negotiator yell "Nag!" at the top of his lungs every time his counterpart, a woman, tried to speak. I called a recess and took him into a side room and told him we would continue only when he could act like—not "be," mind you, simply "act like"—a human. I suggested he take a walk. I watched out the window with some amusement as he stormed feverishly around the park across the street.

You will meet some people who are hard to love, believe me. You must treat them all the same.

Neutrality is something toward which every mediator continually strives. In joint sessions (i.e., when the parties are together), do you ask leading questions of one side and bland queries of the other? Do you let one side ramble and cut the other side off in mid-sentence or urge them to "get to the point"? What if Party A typically shows up early for the negotiations and Party B is always late? If you're punctual, will Party B always find you kibitzing with Party A when they walk in? The caution in chapter 4, to be aware of the unintended signals that you project, applies to mediators as well. Take Party B aside and remind them to be punctual, but don't always let them find you chatting with Party A. Where do you spend your idle time? Party A always sends out for pizza at mealtimes and always has enough for the mediator (but not somehow for Party B). You know Party A's lawyer, and so you sit in his caucus room to visit during idle time.

To be sure, much of a mediator's job is ex parte contact (i.e., contact with only one side), out of earshot of the other. You must gain the parties' trust and confidence. However, it needs to be legitimate and above board. If you're meeting with Party A to discuss their proposal, let Party B know that's what you're doing. During idle time, sit alone unless you're working. Otherwise, Party B will walk past Party A's room and see you in there and will draw the worst possible conclusions. Your credibility is all you have, don't burn it.

Here's a lighthearted but true example of how "optics" matter, of how parties—in this case, both parties—leaped to conclusions over a very innocuous event.

We were in an intensive period of negotiations lasting several days. We were taking only short breaks for meals and an occasional nap. One weekend day, thinking they needed a bit of a respite, I decided to give the parties an extended, several-hour break for dinner. I had time to run home to some of my wife's delicious garlic-rosemary chicken.

I returned as the parties were gathering and returning to their respective caucus rooms. At the end of a long hallway, I ran into the chief negotiator for the union. I knew him well and knew that he was quite a chef. I asked where he had gone to dinner. He answered and returned the question. I told him I had gone home, where I had eaten this delicious dish. He was instantly intrigued and asked me how it was prepared.

141

I began to explain in great detail: First make a paste of the garlic and rosemary (and olive oil, of course), I explained, and then spread it under the skin. As I am wont to do, I was explaining as much with my hands as my words. The chicken is then wrapped in plastic wrap and placed in the refrigerator. I walked him through that step as well. He followed me step by step and was subconsciously mimicking my hand movements.

Unknown to us, the parties were busy shuttling in and out of their caucus rooms at the end of that same hallway. As they did, they kept peering at us down to the opposite end of the hall, obviously in very animated conversation. All they could see was that the mediator and the chief negotiator for the union were in a very intense conversation. They concluded that something must be afoot, something must be happening. And, as anyone who's had my wife's chicken knows, they were right. I learned again the lesson of the importance of optics that night. Luckily, nothing was lost and we all had a few laughs over it, but the point remains: Parties will draw conclusions from the slightest—and unintentional—signal you project. You must project neutrality in all you do.

Parties' hopes and expectations will be raised and dashed—and judgments will be made—on the basis of what you do as a mediator and how you conduct yourself.

Absorb Conflict: In addition to projecting neutrality in all you do, as a mediator you must absorb conflict at all times. Parties might argue with you or try to evoke a reaction. You must betray no emotion, be as expressionless as possible. You can nod to let them know you're listening—and in fact, listen—but you must not react. No one can argue for very long with someone who won't argue with him. It might frustrate a party that you won't engage them, but they will ultimately give up. Don't try to convince them or engage them. Just absorb the angst, the conflict.

I received my first mediation training in law school, in preparation for a summer internship as a conciliator. Some of my classmates and I were trained by a local mediator who was very experienced and seasoned. We did a fair amount of role-playing, and our professor would try to engage the mediator, always with a bit of hostility. The mediator would just stare at him, and just nod and say, "Um-hmm," and continue. At first I thought he was brain dead, but soon I realized he had this incredible calming effect. He listened, heard them out, but didn't engage them. Like Bill Brock in the example in chapter 5, our trainer was respectful, he listened attentively, but he didn't join in discussion of the contentious issues, as much as the parties tried to goad him into it. It was the first time I had seen anyone absorb conflict as an enormously effective tactic. He just soaked it in and left none in the room. Soon, the role-playing parties left the rhetoric and concentrated on the merits of each issue.

Referencing the point made earlier on personality types, you may have a frank and contentious conversation with Party A. If so, you must leave it behind as you shuttle down the hall to see Party B. You can't walk into Party B's room and indicate in any way that Party A has been difficult or is being unreasonable, as they often times will be. You can say anything you want to one party alone, but don't ever reprimand a party within earshot of another. However, once you've reprimanded one party, you must appear to the other party as if nothing has happened.

Parties will frequently complain to you about their counterparts, and will often debate with you the shortcomings of their counterparts' position. First, as already mentioned, they need to tell their counterparts, not you. Second, you can use the opportunity to let them see their counterparts' proposal in a more rational light. Don't be afraid to be a bit of a devil's advocate in describing their counterparts' proposal or point of view in a constructive way. And, make sure you are doing this equally with all sides. This is how you move the parties slowly toward agreement. If you're doing your job well, both parties will tweak you at some point, accusing you of being more partial to their counterpart.

Manage Expectations: Managing expectations is a sometimes near-ministerial but absolutely critical task. Parties' expectations rise in proportion to the time they spend awaiting their counterparts' proposal. If there isn't to be much movement, goes the theory, it won't take long for them to make a counterproposal. However, if there is going to be significant movement on many issues, then they will obviously take more time. Thus, as time passes, expectations rise and often unjustifiably. This speaks more to process than to substance, but if Party B needed to run to an important meeting, better let Party A know they're not off working on the counterproposal, that they've gone elsewhere. Party A might grouse that Party B isn't taking the negotiations seriously, but you can deal with that issue separately. At the moment, you have an expectations problem to manage. If you do, you will keep Party A's expectations in check.

On content, the issue is a bit more delicate. As a mediator you ought not be doing a party's negotiating for them, but to the extent you can play down a party's expectations, you will never have undersold it. And, as mentioned, if you can help put a party's proposal in context in talking to their counterpart, it will help move you closer to an agreement, the object of this exercise.

Here's an example of what can happen when expectations go unmanaged and grow unfettered:

In this particular case, the parties had been negotiating for some time, but an issue of form—not substance—was growing. Party A preferred to make their proposals in short, succinct bullet points. Party B made their proposals fully drafted in contract language. Every time Party A made a proposal, Party B complained that it wasn't in contract language. Party A, of course, was seeking agreement on the principle, the issue, before they expended the effort to put it in a more formal context.

As this was growing as an issue—and since, sooner or later, the agreement would have to be in contract language anyway, I prevailed upon Party A to convert their proposal from bullet points to contract language. This was going to be a time con suming effort, as the lengthy contract covered dozens of issues. I went to the chief negotiator for Party B and told him what was happening. There had been an important "shape of the table" issue that Party A decided they would no longer fight, and Party B should have been relieved. I told Party B this would take a while and said that they could probably take the rest of the day off and we'd reconvene the next day.

To their credit, Party A worked feverishly and were able to accomplish this considerable task by the end of the day. I thus called both parties together the next morning for a joint meeting. I didn't exactly expect a love fest, but I did expect that Party B would be somewhat relieved that Party A had relented on this process issue. When we sat down, Party A pushed a half dozen copies of the proposal across the table, one for each member of the committee in Party B. Party A then began to review it briefly, section by section.

In only a few minutes, several members of Party B's committee exploded. "There's nothing new in here!" they exclaimed, "This is just the same stuff you gave us before—you've not made a single move!" I turned to look at their leader, who avoided my glance. They were unrelenting and irate. "We sat around for an entire day waiting for you to come up with something and all you did was change the language on your old proposal?!?" They stormed out of the room en masse.

I took their leader aside, who stuttered and stammered. He had clearly forgotten to—or chosen not to—tell his colleagues that the company was putting their existing proposal into contract language. Since he never told them, they made the reasonable assumption that a significant passage of time (in this case, an entire day) portended a significant move by Party A. It didn't. But there was nothing anyone could say at that moment to calm the troops, to bring them back from the brink. In short, there was no way to bring their unmanaged expectations back in check.

Walking the fine line between doing the parties' negotiating for them and being an effective mediator includes managing expectations. Imagine that Party A has made a proposal that Party B has examined and rejected out of hand. Party B has asked you for a few hours to reassess their position before they meet again with you or with Party A. You'd better let Party A know what's going on. Otherwise, given the passage of time, Party A will assume that Party B has taken their proposal seriously and is ready to respond. When they meet together for the first time, any explosion will be much worse unless Party A knows what to expect, gets their own expectations in check.

Most of the problems with expectations are related to time, specifically the passage of time and the accompanying rise in hope as outlined above. On content, the role of the mediator is a bit trickier and involves an aspect of managing expectations that might be referred to as "reality checking." This is a fine line to walk, but it is important. In terms of the content of a party's proposal, you ought not characterize that with the other side (i.e., as sufficient, insufficient, good, or bad); nor should you characterize it or editorialize on it with the party making the proposal. Don't inject your opinion when you're tinkering at the margins on a particular proposal.

However, in the extremes you may need to inject yourself, again, to "reality check," to put the parties in the right frame of mind to settle. But you'd better be accurate, noninflammatory, cool, reasoned—and right.

Let me go back to my old friend and colleague, Maggie Jacobsen, She was as effective at "reality checking" as anyone I've seen. In "pattern bargaining," parties in a given industry tend to negotiate agreements that follow the pattern of others negotiated in that same industry. It is called an industry pattern. Once the pattern is set, it is rare, if not extraordinary, for someone in that industry to break it. One time, Maggie was sitting down with a negotiating committee that had unreasonably high hopes for their negotiation. She had met with them several times, and the negotiations had begun in earnest. There was no progress because their expectations were not even visible—much less attainable—from where their counterpart sat. After several week of unproductive negotiations, Maggie had to sit down with the group and tell them that, as she said, they needed to "get on the same planet" as everyone else. Within the general confines of a pattern agreement, there's some room for movement, to tailor a particular agreement to the needs of that particular workforce, but this group wasn't even close enough to the other side to talk. She had to talk to them (alone, of course), lay down the law, and let them know there would be no agreement as long as their expectations remained extra-terrestrial. It took a few days for the admonition to sink in, but ultimately it sobered them and they were able to reach a deal, which fairly closely tracked the industry pattern.

This is admittedly a fine line. Mediators are not management consultants. They are not there to give advice. They must be without conscience (see below). But in some instances, as part of managing expectations, you must make sure both parties are at least on the same planet. Closer than that, mediators should avoid giving advice, but if it's possible, you should caution them—always out of the earshot of the other party—that their expectations are not realistic. If they are merely posturing, don't worry, but if after a decent passage of time they aren't moving off of these positions, you need to at least get them in the same area code. Don't fine-tune beyond that or you'll be second-guessing and doing their negotiating for them.

In sum, if Party A is responding to only two of fifteen items, let Party B know. In terms of what is in those proposals, don't characterize them as good or bad. As far as the other party is concerned, you'll be wrong almost all the time.

Which leads us to our next rule for mediators.

Check Your Conscience at the Door: The ideal mediator is a person without conscience. To a mediator, the truth is only those things to which the parties agree. A mediator's job is to help the parties reach agreement, period. It is up to the parties to decide whether an agreement is sufficient from their perspective. It is similar to the American system of jurisprudence. You can't let the lawyers decide who is guilty and who is innocent. That is for the jury to decide. Similarly, as a mediator, you must be a fierce defender of the process and of all things impartial. On content, you must leave it to the parties' own judgment as to whether a particular final deal is good enough for them. In sophisticated bargaining, parties usually come armed with lawyers and professional negotiators anyway. These folks are grown-ups. They should be able to know whether they have a good deal or not. That's not the mediator's job. If it were, what would he use as a yardstick? Is this deal fair to labor? Fair to management? Can this person afford this deal? Is this industry standard? Are they realizing a sufficient profit? It is not for the mediator to make any of these judgments.

In any mediation, there are at least two positions, one belonging to Party A and one belonging to Party B. In multiparty cases, there are even more points of view around the table. There ought not be one more (i.e., the mediator's position). Mediators are human, that's true, but they are not entitled to a point of view—or at least not entitled to voice it or advance it—in any negotiation. Every mediator with any degree of experience has seen parties agree to outrageous and often ill conceived items. Mediators must keep a poker face and move on to the next item. Remember that the object is to make the list of open items shorter and the list of agreed items longer. If parties agree to something—however bizarre it may be—put it in the "Agreed" pile and move on.

In one case, there was one person on each side of the table who fancied himself the Nobel Laureate in economics. While grappling with the issue of a retroactive pay increase, both agreed to peg the increases to the Consumer Price Index (CPI) for the two years since the last raise. The CPI is a number easily ascertainable with one phone call or one mouse click to the Bureau of Labor Statistics (BLS). However, both of these fellows decided they didn't need BLS, since they knew what the CPI was.

Party A said the CPI for the two years was 2.9 percent and 2.4 percent, respectively. His counterpart with Party B replied in the most condescending terms, saying that he was incorrect, that the true numbers were exactly reverse (i.e., 2.4 percent for the first year and 2.9 percent for the second). Party A, he opined haughtily, must have transposed the numbers. Party A indeed backed off and deferred to Party B, and Party B's numbers were written into the agreement. I should note that the contract did not reference the CPI, just these two percentages. We initialed the section and moved on.

Out of curiosity, about a week later and after the agreement had been concluded, I called BLS myself. As it turns out, neither one of them was right. The correct numbers were 2.9 percent and 2.7 percent, respectively.

There are some mediators who might be shocked at my behavior here and who would see themselves as having an obligation to inject themselves into this debate. I saw my role quite differently. Again, if the agreement referenced the CPI specifically, it would have been incumbent upon me to make sure the numbers were right, so that we'd have a full and solid agreement at day's end. However, in this case, they were writing in the percentages. Both men held positions of great responsibility in their respective organizations. If it mattered that much, either one of them could have called to glean the correct number. They didn't and it was their error, if an error at all. They wrote in the numbers and agreed to those percentages, and that's where it ended. It was not for me to check them or to reopen an item—much less an agreement—after it was closed.

In sum, you must leave the parties to their own devices, let them make their own mistakes. You can't save them from themselves, can't stop them from making a bad deal. You need to keep moving the parties toward agreement, without regard to who might be getting the better deal. In virtually every case, there will be a fairly equal amount of give and take. Every now and then you'll see the exception to the rule, but it is not your job to ensure justice and fairness in terms of the elements of any final agreement. Your only job is to help them get a deal.

Here is one final scenario on this point, where a mediator's lack of conscience let the parties stumble into a deal, for better or worse.

I had unsuccessfully tried to mediate an agreement in one case, and the parties had entered into a fairly protracted strike. I kept in touch with them, but it was clear that both sides wanted some time to exercise their economic muscle, to see who might blink first. One day, a few weeks later, I picked up that day's edition of the industry trade publication, which featured a wide-ranging interview with the CEO of that company. The headline screamed that in the course of the interview and the discussion of the strike, he had offered the striking employees the same contract enjoyed by one of their major competitors. It was big news, since this was one of the longest strikes the industry had seen in some time. This particular company was a time zone or two away from me, so I waited a decent interval, then called the company negotiator.

"What's going on?" I asked expectantly.

He was without a clue. "What are you talking about?" he asked. I told him of the article on the front page. "Oh, that," he said, almost bored. "That's nothing. It was just an off-handed comment made by our CEO in the interview and they (the press) just blew it all out of proportion."

I wished him well, hung up, and immediately called the union. I had worked with their negotiator many times before, and we had a good relationship. It was clear when they answered the phone at the union office that in spite of the early hour, it was a beehive of activity. They put me through immediately to their chief negotiator.

"Hey!" I said, "How's it going?"

He was polite, but fairly curt. "I can't talk to you now," he said hurriedly, "We're crunching numbers."

I asked what he meant. He told me that since the CEO had offered the competitor's agreement to them—via the press—they were busy running those numbers, to see how they might fare under that agreement. *"Oh,"* I said. I wished him well also and hung up.

Later that day, the union telephoned the CEO and accepted the offer he made on the front page of the trade newspaper. There was nothing the CEO could do, since the offer, whether it was adequately thought through or not, had been so publicly made. The strike was over. Incidentally, within six months, that CEO was forced to resign, in part due to the continuing financial slide of the company and in part because of residual ill will among top management and his board of directors for what they considered to be this major faux pas.

A different mediator might have told the union that in fact the company did not intend to make that proposal, but in my view, that was not my job. Clearly the parties should have communicated, but they didn't. The company negotiator should have immediately conveyed to the union that this was not a real offer, it was just idle chit-chat by the CEO, but he didn't. When I discovered they were working on the proposal, I didn't feel it was my place to intervene. Also, it wasn't a mistake of such colossal proportions that it was accomplished by fraud or sleight of hand. It was a relatively comparable contract, and in fact it took the union all day to calculate its impact before they could accept, that is, before they realized that it would result in a net gain for their members.

Ultimately, these guys were grown-ups. They had dug their own hole. It was not for me to pull them out once they backed themselves into a deal, even if it was one they wouldn't have volunteered. In the purest sense, the top executive of the company made what looked like an offer and the union accepted. Offer, acceptance, game, set, match.

Bottom line: Check your conscience at the door and let the chips—and the parties—fall where they may.

Don't Make Mediator's Proposals: Recall the point made above, that is, that in every negotiation, you have as many positions as you have parties and maybe even more. You ought not complicate it by adding a position for the mediator. The mediator is not entitled to a position.

Yet, like the apple in the Garden of Eden, mediator's proposals are incredibly tempting, especially to the novice. It is the novice's curse, because it is the mediator as negotiator (rather than the other way around), the impatient mediator, the mediator who is having a "Eureka!" moment, who sees where the parties may finish and wants to move them there hastily. Think about it: a mediator's proposal is really the mediator's best guess of the mid-point between the two parties. If you miss your guess and draw that mid-point too close to Party A, you've lost the confidence of Party B. Recall that patience is your friend. The trick is in moving the parties slowly toward agreement, slowly getting them used to accepting alternatives to their proposals, putting them in a frame of mind to compromise. Don't rush it. It will almost always backfire, as you'll see, except in one very narrow instance, which will be covered later.

I made a mediator's proposal in my very first case, against the advice of our most senior mediator. I cut this one a bit too close to the union and the company blew their stack, while the union said they'd "reluctantly" accept it. What was I to do with that—one acceptance and one rejection? I stayed in the case and ultimately gained an agreement, but I was wounded.

I was so chastened by that experience that I never tried it again until almost five years later, when it appeared totally irresistible at the end of what had been a very high-profile and contentious case. It was about 10:30 P.M. before a midnight deadline and I was working in tandem with another, much more senior and seasoned mediator. We were worried that the parties would not be able to conclude an agreement before their hard midnight deadline and they were down to only a few issues. Against his better judgment (and because of my constant hectoring), my mediator partner worked with me to draw up a mediator's proposal covering the last few open issues.

The company was in dire financial straits and thus one of their proposals was a pay freeze, which was obviously opposed strongly by the union. In the careful balancing my fellow mediator and I did in drafting our document, our proposal, we granted this to the company, in return for some item (which I don't recall) that was coveted by the union and equally opposed by the company. We dutifully completed our work. As we had no access to a computer there in the wee hours, we wrote out the proposal and made copies for each side.

As we were ready to call the parties together to break the logjam and present our proposal, the company told us they were ready to make a move. They did, and it broke the impasse, and the few remaining issues were settled. Indeed, as in our proposal, the union had accepted the pay freeze as part of the final package. In the final meeting, just minutes before midnight, the parties sat in the room together, reviewing the final agreement and readying it for signature.

The chief negotiator for the union had one question. "I just want to be clear," he said, "By 'pay freeze' here, you mean we're not going to get any increases, but we'll continue to move up the scale, right?"

In most union contracts there is a pay scale that pegs pay to years of service. Every year, on your anniversary date, you move up another level—a higher level of pay—on the scale. In addition, in each negotiation there is typically a general wage increase, of, for example, 3 percent. That increases the amounts in each step of the scale by 3 percent. In other words, an employee's pay can rise in two ways: by moving up to the next level of the pay scale and through general wage increases. In this company, they had a pay scale of about ten years in length.

What the union leader was trying to clarify was that there would be no 3 percent or other general wage increase, but that an eight-year employee, for example, would still go to step 9 on their anniversary date.

The company blanched. "No," they replied tersely. They intended to freeze everyone's pay—to give no general wage increase and to freeze everyone at their current step of the pay scale. Under their proposal, as they intended it, there would be no increase in any employee's pay during at least part of this agreement.

A huge argument ensued, but there was enough momentum toward a deal at that point that they somehow settled the issue. I say "somehow" because I think my fellow mediator and I might have passed out, having seen our professional lives pass before our eyes.

Think about it. In our bold and brave "mediator's proposal," we wrote the words, "pay freeze," since those words had been discussed back and forth by the parties for weeks, if not longer. They all thought they were working from the same assumptions, but in fact, they were working from quite different assumptions. Had we offered our proposal and had the parties accepted, either at that moment or some time later, one of them would have asked us that pay-scale question, and we would have had no answer at all on one of the most crucial and critical issues in the whole negotiation. What would we have done? On whose side would we have come down? The truth of the matter is that we had no idea what we meant, nor were the parties sure of what they had intended. Had this proposal been delivered to the parties by a third hand—namely the mediators'—then the re-

sponsibility for lack of clarity on this most important point would have resided with us. We mediators would have been in the anomalous position of waiting and hoping for the parties to bail us out. We dodged the bullet. But for a nanosecond, we were prepared to make this proposal and would have been scorched as a result. There almost certainly would have been a strike, caused by none other than the mediators.

There is only one circumstance in which a mediator should ever make a mediator's proposal, and that is when someone from both sides—with authority to make the deal—has seen it in advance and blessed it. Even then, in most of those cases, once you propose it, both sides will publicly criticize it in front of their colleagues but will reluctantly accept it, after appropriate protest, of course. It's all part of the game, not to worry. If it gets you to a deal, let them protest. There are also techniques used by some mediators where they draft a document and let both parties tinker with it and critique it and pass it back and forth in a process all its own. If you learn that process and find it helpful, use it, but even here the parties are seeing the document and are writing it and it's malleable. The typical mediator's proposal is a static document dropped on the parties by an impatient mediator. Other than the one, narrow, and very orchestrated exception noted herein, stifle all urges—and there will be many—to make a mediator's proposal. They are incredibly tempting, but they are a novice's folly. They almost always fail.

Create the Atmosphere for an Agreement: It is the mediator's job to create the atmosphere for an agreement. Left to their own devices, the parties will rely on their baser instincts; they will doubt that an agreement is possible; they will create and foment enmity; they will go on and on with no end in sight. A mediator must resist and indeed make every effort to reverse

156

these natural trends. The creation of the right atmosphere is part science, part voodoo, but all very real. Some suggestions follow.

Inevitability. At the outset, a mediator might tell the parties that they will reach a deal at some point. This is especially true in labor negotiations. Whether peacefully in advance of the contract deadline or after a long and bitter strike, the people in that room are going to have to sit down and see their way clear to an agreement. This is only slightly less so in the commercial setting. In mediation that precedes litigation, there is a slightly different wrinkle, that is, statistically speaking, the vast majority of cases will not make it all the way to a jury. At some point short of a verdict, these parties will sit down and hammer out a deal, a settlement. In the case of litigation, the more time that passes, the more it costs the parties in legal fees, an incentive all its own. Sometimes at the beginning of a negotiation it is hard for the parties to see their way clear to a settlement, but a mediator should make the point that the great likelihood is that they will settle, and they ought to do it sooner rather than later and save themselves all some heartache. In family and other mediation, the same is true. One way or another, this same group of people will have to figure it out. Also, remind them that momentum, the natural order of things, favors an agreement, as noted in chapter 5. The clear odds are in favor of a settlement, of peace.

Create a sense of teamwork. Some mediators begin a mediation by sitting on one side of the table and seating the parties together on the other side of the table, facing the mediator. It is a physical manifestation of a central point, that is, that they are in the same boat, they share a common problem. It helps them focus less on what divides them than on what unites them. Reference all the points in chapter 3 about conflict resolution. The same tactics you might use as a negotiator can be employed by a mediator and vice-versa. If the parties won't establish common ground or set a positive tone on their own (and most of them won't) then the mediator must do it for them.

Defuse tension. In any dispute, there is a level of tension. Depending on the nature of the dispute, there can be an enormous amount of tension in the room. It saps energy and distracts the parties from their real goal. If there is more tension when the parties are in the same room, separate them. Perhaps you need to operate with only a small group, one or two from each side, in one room. Whatever dynamic you find that lessens the tension, use it. Don't be afraid to use humor with the parties, and encourage them to use it with one another.

In one dispute, we were meeting on a Sunday, with everyone from both committees in attendance. The humorist Dave Barry had written a lengthy and hilarious column, which had run in the paper that day, on political life in Washington. The company lawyer happened to read it in an idle moment and could be heard guffawing from any point in the office. When he had finished reading the article, he happened to hand it to one of the people on the union committee, who read it with the same reaction. We had enough idle time that day, and that piece made the rounds. Whichever side was not working on a proposal had the Dave Barry article and someone new was reading it, to gales of laughter. The various parties kept referring to the piece throughout the day and indeed throughout the rest of the negotiations. I made sure everyone had seen it. It had the twin benefits of lifting everyone's mood and giving them all some common ground.

Mediators should employ all the tactics of any good negotiator to defuse tension. Recall the example in chapter 3 of the young woman who complimented the car dealer on his honesty. At times, one party, meeting alone with you, might note appreciation for the other party's difficulty, or express gratitude (if begrudging) at some moves, perhaps, that their counterpart has made in their direction. If so, don't be afraid to convey that quietly to their counterparts. You'll be amazed at how surprised they will be. It is all too easy for people to equate business differences with personal differences. Disputes are not warm, fuzzy things. They're uncomfortable and people feel them quite personally. As a mediator, if you have a way to convey to one side or the other that it's not personal, or that the other party has been positive in some way, let them know. It will do wonders for the atmosphere, and make it easier for them to see the other side in a more positive light.

Create momentum. While there is always some degree of momentum in favor of a deal, sometimes a mediator must create some momentum of his own. If a negotiation is particularly lengthy or protracted, it is easy for the parties to become complacent, to work a straight nine-to-five day (or less), and to take their time. If there is no natural deadline, you often need to create one. While it is true that parties can use the time to build a relationship, there are occasions where enough time has passed for them to build the relationship many times over, yet no end date is in sight. These are the circumstances where a mediator needs to create some sense of urgency with the parties (i.e., where the negotiation is open-ended).

The easiest way to create some sense of urgency is to throw out the clock (i.e., begin working around the clock). This does help the parties realize that this is serious business and that they'd better become more focused. Mediators can also set deadlines, but they are under the same burdens as negotiators—for example, if they set artificial deadlines and don't honor them, every future deadline is useless.

Without some sense of urgency, the parties have all day to ponder, to pursue the perfect solution, to tinker with words ad nauseam. The adage is true that work will expand to fill the time allowed. Shrinking the time frame a bit will focus the parties' minds and force them to make some decisions they might not have made otherwise.

There is also a mediation truism you should be aware of when working around the clock: Human nature seems weakest between 3 A.M. and 4 A.M. People are tired then, and it seems that all body clocks sink at that time. Your chances for a deal are better as resistance slips. However, the corollary is also true: If you don't have a deal by the time the sun comes up, send everyone home for a nap. The light of reason, which the sun brings, and the "buyer's remorse" are palpable. If signatures are not on that paper by dawn, forget it until another day.

Remember that negotiators can employ some of these points as tactics when trying to absorb conflict and move their counterparts to agreement.

In mediating one very high-profile case, I employed all the above tactics and more. First and most important, the parties had been negotiating through the press and were only heightening the tension and increasingly painting themselves into a corner with no way out, thus making settlement all the more difficult. I did a few things. I first contacted the parties and told them we'd be negotiating in earnest beginning the next day, with a one-week push. That, I hoped, was going to create some sense of urgency. I told them to stop negotiating through the press, and I called a press blackout on the negotiations. These blackouts, a common mediator's tool in high-profile cases, are only as good as the parties let them be. As mentioned before, a mediator has no independent authority to enforce any of these demands, but for the moment, in this one case, the parties complied. Next, I said we'd be moving to an undisclosed location, which I told them I didn't expect to see in the papers. We picked a small town just outside of Washington, D.C. This way, they would be sequestered from family and friends and a host of ancillary people who were stirring the pot, and it would give them the feeling of being free of all distractions and hopefully focused as well. Once we arrived, we worked around the clock for days on end and finally concluded an agreement, but it took every trick we had in our bag to get there.

Incidentally, this case was also the occasion for some comic relief amid all the tension. I had read the riot act to both parties, threatening to take their lives if they so much as uttered the site of our meetings to anyone. The hotel we picked was located only a hundred yards from the freeway, in a town where many of that company's employees lived. As I drove up to the hotel, I could see on the hotel marquee a giant sign welcoming the company and the union negotiating committee. As I walked into the hotel lobby, the union and company negotiator, both in a state of high agitation were waiting for me. "If we're going to be in an 'undisclosed location,' they demanded, don't you think they oughta at least take us off the goddam marquee?" I nodded and walked over to the desk. For this little hotel in this little town, this was the biggest thing that had ever happened to them and they were so proud. I felt bad for them, but worried more about attracting unwanted attention. They changed the marquee.

In the last section of this chapter, we will examine two final points. One is the age-old, "less filling versus tastes great" debate of whether mediation is an art or a science and the implications of the question—and the answer—for mediators. The second is on the proper use of a mediator, that is, if you are a negotiator who has occasion to use a mediator, what is their highest and best use?

Mediation: Art versus Science: At the core of this debate is the question of precisely what and how much is expected of a mediator on a particular case. The artistes would say that it is the parties' job to be versed in the issues and the accompanying numbers. They are the ones who need to know the industry involved (e.g., the steel business, the real estate business, or the divorce business). The mediator is a facilitator, a combination high priest and sorcerer, there to make sure the conversation stays productive and doesn't deteriorate into name-calling, and finger-pointing, and other assorted destructive patterns.

The scientists, however, would say that a mediator's job is to know everything the parties know, or to learn everything he can about, for instance, the steel, real estate, and divorce industries; that he has to cast a careful eye on the parties and their proposals; that he should check the parties' numbers and offer specific and concrete ideas for solving the issues.

Most mediators, not surprisingly, come down somewhere in between these two views, although there are mediators who subscribe to each of these views. While it is true that it is for the parties to know their respective businesses and proposals, the preferred course is for the mediator to have some familiarity with the topic, the industry that is the substance of the dispute. Beyond that, they should let the parties do the negotiating, but stay with them on numbers and keep an eye on the details.

Recall the discussion on "awfulisms" in chapter 4. The parties discussed their industry but were so busy arguing that they missed the fact that they were arguing over an impossibility, given the nature of their particular operations. A mediator must let the parties negotiate, but must also pay attention to the details of the various proposals, which may be causing impediments to agreement.

It was the day before the strike deadline when the union came to me and told me they were going home, that no deal would be reached that night. We had been making slow but steady progress and I couldn't understand what accounted for their pessimism. They explained that they were discouraged because—on a contract with a total value of only about $4 million—they were still $1.2 million apart. I couldn't imagine why they were still that far apart. I thought they had cut their differences to under $1 million earlier that same day and that some other issues had been settled in the interim. How on earth, I wondered, did the gap climb back over the $1 million mark?

I called the lead negotiators from both sides into a room with me and we went over the numbers. Everyone was tired and the union negotiator was sketching the numbers out on a piece of paper, under the watchful eye of the company negotiator and me. Sure enough, his tally came to a $1.2 million difference between their two proposals, and I could feel the pessimism in the room grow. The company negotiator checked his numbers again and just shook his head. I finally took the piece of paper and examined it while they talked. I was virtually certain they weren't that far apart. Sure enough, upon examining the numbers, I saw that the union negotiator had mistakenly added a $600,000 item twice, thereby doubling the distance between them. In an instant, a seemingly insurmountable $1.2 million gap became an eminently soluble $600,000 gap.

In short, mediation is one part art, one part science. A mediator needs to keep stride with the parties on substance, but at the same time not become bogged down in minutiae. The mediator's job is to keep prodding, keep moving the parties together. The mediator doesn't need to come up with all the solutions but does need to keep pressing the parties to come up with creative solutions of their own making.

The ideal case for a mediator is one in which he or she does some heavy lifting and keeps a watchful eye on the process, but strikes the right balance between intervention and nonintervention, between art and science. The best mediators stay at the margins of the process, nudging the parties back toward the center and forward.

The difference between my first mediation case for the U.S. government and my last was the difference between night and day. In my first case, I dominated the process. I lorded over the parties and constantly worked to come up with my own solutions to their problems. When the case finally settled—in spite of me, I think—I was a bit irked that the parties did not heap praise and adulation on me. They said their "thank-you's," but that was it. I felt that I never received the proper level of appreciation from the parties for all my hard work. Their relationship at the end of the case was no better than it had been when we began except that they had a new agreement, albeit the result of a difficult birth.

Toward the end of my last case, I positioned the parties in rooms across the hall from one another and let them run the process. I sat at the end of the (long) hallway, mostly reading and biding my time. Every now and then, one of the parties would come walking by me. "Where are you going?" I'd ask.

"We're going home," they'd say, telling me they'd reached an impasse.

"Get back in there," I'd say, and convene the principals from both sides to see where they had broken down. I'd work with them to brainstorm, to get back on track, then take my perch back at the end of the hallway again. To be sure, there was no

shortage of heavy lifting for me. It was the case where I discovered the mathematical error and the case where the parties kept moving "the rock" back and forth on one another. It helped, too, that both negotiators were very seasoned. It took a fair amount of my time and attention, but mostly it was spent at the edge, keeping the parties between the lines, making sure they didn't quit.

When the negotiation was over, at the last session I sat at the end of the table as the parties exchanged very sincere praise and gratitude for their counterparts' efforts. It had moved 180 degrees from where we had started. After they added their signatures to the tentative agreement, they all stood up and gathered and shook hands and talked and joked good-naturedly. While they stood talking, I remember gathering up my papers and quietly exiting the room and walking back to my office, feeling great. Both parties called me the next day to thank me, and I appreciated the calls. But the most important thing to me was that they had made the agreement, not I. I had kept them moving, but they made the agreement. In the process, they built a relationship with one another that heretofore had not existed.

After all those years, I felt that I finally got it right.

How to Make Use of a Mediator: At one time or another, as a negotiator you may need the services of a mediator or find yourself involved in a case where a mediator is present. There are very few people who know how to use a mediator effectively. There are really two extremes. Those at one end treat the mediator with total distrust, as a complete outsider. They relegate the mediator to the role of note-taker, if that. Those at the other end of the spectrum embrace the mediator, involve him in all aspects of their discussions, and basically use him as another negotiator. Neither extreme is desirable.

Negotiators often ask mediators for strategic advice. After all, they are as familiar with the parties and the issues as the negotiators themselves. However, as mediator, you must keep in mind that you are not a management consultant, you're a mediator. Strategy is for the parties to decide. Mediators are there to help narrow differences between the sides. This is sometimes a fine line, admittedly, but a mediator must be careful not to be part of one side's strategy, only part of the solution.

Neither should the mediator be relegated to the role only of note-taker and chief copier. Often, the parties use the mediator to courier proposals back and forth to the other side. If you are not making fuller use of your mediator than this, you're wasting a valuable resource. How should you make use of a mediator? Here are some thoughts:

- A mediator first and foremost can help you put things in context and hopefully help you keep a level head when the going gets tough.
- A mediator can help a negotiator float an idea, like a "what if." You can even test out different permutations and combinations, for example, "If we give them X and Y, will they give us Z?" A good mediator can handle all of this.
- Mediators can help to keep the negotiations on track, keep the parties focused and moving forward.
- You should also use the mediator as a resource. If he has some experience, chances are he's seen this issue, this predicament before. How did others deal with this? What are other creative solutions to your particular problem? A good mediator will probably volunteer these things, but if not, you may want to prompt him.
- Your mediator can also help set the pace of negotiations. If

things are moving too slowly, he can help you get it jump-started.

- A mediator can be used to reality-check you and the other side. If you have a proposal, you may want to ask the mediator's opinion of how it might be viewed by the other side. If it's his best guess that it'll be poorly received, you may want to rework it or rethink making it at all.

Again, the mediator is not there to do your negotiating for you. With the active involvement of a mediator, it's easy for the parties to sit back and just let the mediator do all the work. A good mediator will not let himself be used in this way, because he knows that the most important result is one where the parties have built a relationship along the way. You don't build a relationship by having someone else do your negotiating for you.

Basically, keep in mind that the mediator is a resource, not a clerk. Any good mediator doesn't mind making copies or making the coffee, if it helps get the job done. Don't use your mediator just to set meetings and take notes. Use him to help you gain an agreement.

Epilogue
The Gym Wall

I have spent a fair amount of time as a mediator. I have spent even more time thinking about mediation and speaking and lecturing on the topic. The process of negotiation and dispute resolution is one I find fascinating. As mentioned at the outset, all disputes share common pathologies and their similarities never cease to amaze me, regardless of what the underlying conflict may be, from world affairs to family matters.

After years of working in this field and studying and thinking about these issues, I attended my nephew's elementary-school basketball game on a rainy winter Saturday afternoon. In the gym were some rules on how to handle conflict. I took out my pen and scribbled them down. They reinforce the adage from Robert Fulghum's famous book mentioned in the introduction, that everything you need to know you learn in kindergarten.

After years in this field, I think they captured the essence of it all. Out of the mouths of babes. . . .

On one wall were the key elements of dealing with a difficult person or avoiding conflict. It said, "When Someone Bothers Me, I Can:

1. *Ignore them*
2. *Walk away*
3. *Speak in a friendly voice*
4. *Speak in a clear voice*
5. *Go for help.*

I smiled to myself, recalling my first year as a mediator, which I spent stranded in element number 5. It seems I was always going for help, having failed miserably at calming the various beasts around me. The other elements pertain to all negotiators and were strikingly similar to some of the tenets I had developed. Number one I view as "noise and rhetoric are part of the process." You must ignore it and not engage it. For those who must make a deal, you can't walk away, but you must certainly "speak in a friendly voice" (i.e., set the tone, establish common ground) and "speak in a firm voice" (i.e., let your counterpart know your principles—what you can and can't compromise).

On the opposite wall of the gym was a series of posters horizontally set, as a continuum of dispute resolution. They were labeled as follows:

1. *I want . . .*
2. *I feel . . .*
3. *The reason is . . .*
4. *My understanding of you is . . .*
5. *Maybe we should try . . .*
6. *Let's shake on it!*

These further reinforced the rules I had already distilled. "I want" and "I feel" mean knowing your priorities and having some empathy, letting your counterpart know the reasons behind your position. Similarly with, "the reason is," that is, selling your proposal, not just throwing it out there. "Maybe we should try" is brainstorming, plain and simple, and the negotiator as mediator. It's your job to brainstorm, to find a way. Finally, the deal concludes with, "Let's shake on it!" and the relationship is cemented.

These struck me as so important that I've posted them on my website: www.workingstrategicsinc.com. Next time you find yourself in a dispute, keep these near you and refer to them often. Like the pre-teens for which they were intended, you will find that they will serve you well and will help you steer through almost any dispute.

Appendix
Bargaining Scenario

You are the vice president of labor relations for XYZ Corp., a Fortune 500 company that manufactures widgets. You report to the senior vice president of labor relations who, in turn, reports to the CEO.

XYZ Corp. is in an industry that has been hard-hit by its competition and has lost hundreds of millions of dollars over the past several years. The CEO, fearing a continued slide, cashed in his stock options this year totaling some $15 million.

The company's pay has always lagged somewhat behind other companies in the widget industry, as have its earnings.

You are engaged in bargaining with the International Association of Widget Makers (IAWM). They seek parity with other IAWM locals throughout the industry. The salient issues remaining on the table, and the relative positions, are as follows:

Pay: The company is asking for a wage freeze for a year, followed by a 1 percent increase for four more years. If pressed, you can probably agree to two years of a 2 percent raise, and three years of a 3 percent increase, but your current position is as stated above (Freeze-1 percent-1 percent-1 percent-1 percent). The union, seeking to regain "industry standards," is seeking only a three-year agreement, with a 7 percent increase each year.

Health Benefits: In response to rising heath care costs, the company is seeking to increase the employee contribution from the current $10/month to $30/month. The union wants status quo (i.e., to keep the current $10/month rate).

Duration: The company wants a five-year agreement in order to gain labor stability and to lock in (lower) costs for as many years as possible. The union wants a three-year agreement in the hopes that the company's fortunes will reverse (i.e., improve), and thus enable them to negotiate a better deal at that time.

Wild Cards: The lack of labor peace at your company has given Wall Street the jitters, and the stock is falling. The board of directors is meeting next week, and if you have a tentative agreement by then, you will probably be canonized. If not, you may well be publicly shot. You are scheduled to make a presentation to the full board on the first day of their meeting. Also, tempers are flaring on the property, and an irate IAWM (Tom Jefferson) punched a supervisor last week after the supervisor tried to discipline the worker for being late. The employee has been fired and has filed a grievance protesting the firing.

Index